Our Debt to Greece and Rome

EDITORS
George Depue Hadzsits, Ph.D.

David Moore Robinson, Ph.D., LL.D.

AESCHYLUS
Naples, National Museum

AESCHYLUS & SOPHOCLES
THEIR WORK AND INFLUENCE

BY

J. T. SHEPPARD, M.A., LITT.D.

COOPER SQUARE PUBLISHERS, INC.
NEW YORK
1963

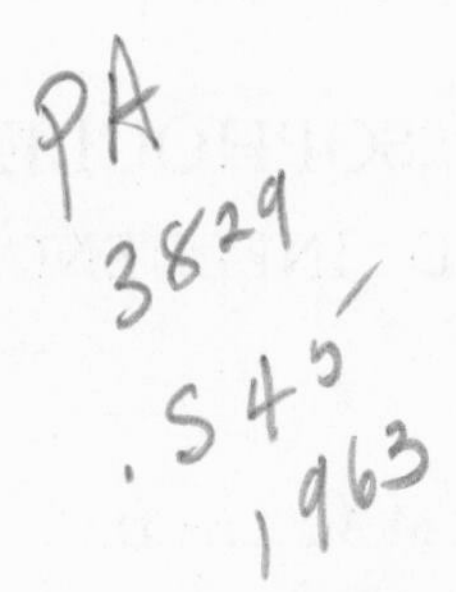

Published 1963 by Cooper Square Publishers, Inc.
59 Fourth Avenue, New York 3, N. Y.
Library of Congress Catalog Card No. 63-10270

PRINTED IN THE UNITED STATES OF AMERICA

CONTENTS

Part I. Antiquity

Part II. Modern Influences

PART I
ANTIQUITY

PART I
ANTIQUITY

I. THE WORK OF AESCHYLUS

AS HOMER knew, there were dancing-places in prehistoric Greece.[1] Odysseus marvelled at the twinkling feet of the Phaeacian dancers while a minstrel sang of Ares and of Aphrodite. Centuries before Aeschylus was born, in this combination of a ballad with a dance, there was a germ of drama.

Homer's *Iliad* was a new creation, made by his genius out of old material.[2] The tales of Troy, founded on truth, but enriched already first by singers, then by reciters, came to him with a tradition of a simple, but flexible narrative technique. He so refashioned the material that the whole siege became a background for one tragic theme, the Wrath of Achilles, its inception from King Agamemnon's insult, its hardening into perverse obsession, when Achilles in his turn rejected Agamemnon's offer of amends, its transformation to a passionate consuming lust for vengeance when Patroclus had been killed, and the final resolution into harmony when the hero listened to the prayers of Priam. The large symmetry of pattern, the balanced grouping of subordinate incident, the distribution of the images and similes, woven like threads of colour in the main design, made the poem an acknowledged masterpiece of form, from which the later poets learnt their art.

In the lyrical age, the poetry of speech, enriched beyond imagination by Homer, was wedded to elaborate mimetic dancing and a musical accompaniment subtle in mode and rhythm. The steps and gestures of the dance, and the melodies of harp and flute, were linked with words by poet-composers. Sometimes the dancers sang together; sometimes in groups. Sometimes a leader sang alone, the rest interpreting the words by motion. In the seventh century Alcman made a ballet-lyric for a choir of Spartan ladies on the meeting of Nausicaa and Odysseus. In the sixth, the Sicilian Stesichorus narrated in this form the home-coming of Agamemnon, his murder, and the vengeance taken by his son. Leaders and solo-dancers in such performances were the ancestors of tragic actors. But the decisive step to dramatic character and plot was not yet taken.

Two forms of lyric may have contributed more than the rest: the Dithyramb, which celebrated, and perhaps symbolically re-enacted, the birth and death and triumph of the nature-god, Dionysus; and the Dirge, intended to propitiate Heroes by the narration, and perhaps the mimic reproduction at their graves, of their feats, their trials, and their glorious deaths. Such performances, arranged by men like Thespis, no longer as ritual, but as public entertainments, have left their mark on Attic Tragedy.

But Aeschylus was the creator of European drama, ransacking a mass of experience, but choosing, shaping, dominating his material. Born in 525 B.C., when Peisistratus had made Athens a home of poetry and music, he heard the rhapsodes declaiming Homer. In choral lyric, at the festivals of Dionysus, poets and musicians vied with one another for his pleasure: and he saw the crude performances, rustic in plot and metre and diction, half-grotesque, half-solemn, with which the followers of Thespis charmed a simple audience. He exploited all these opportunities. 'He first used two actors instead of one,' says Aristotle.[3] If so, he was the first who made dramatic presentation, with the play of character on character, effective. 'He reduced the part assigned to Chorus, and made dialogue the protagonist,' and for dialogue he used, instead of the old dancing metre, the more dignified, more eloquent and flexible iambic. Experience has justified his choice. From his full-toned trimeters descend both Racine's Alexandrine and our own blank verse. He ennobled Tragedy by choice of high heroic themes, by the invention of the trilogy, as a spacious form for rich and varied presentation, by the elaboration of costumes, masks and setting, and above all by the forging of a copious imaginative diction, full of colour, and dramatic. 'He first,' says Aristophanes, 'built in strength the tragic phrase, and robed in stateliness what had been — the tragic trumpery.'

The *Suppliants,* a specimen of his early work, confirms this ancient tradition. Here the element of ballet-lyric still predominates. The fifty Danaids, pursued by their detested suitors, take refuge in a sacred grove near Argos, and claim sanctuary as descendants of the Argive princess Io. In a delicious ritual of dance and song they recall her strange adventures. They picture her gathering flowers in the Argive meadows, wooed by Zeus, transformed into a cow, tormented by the gadfly, and driven in a wild career to Egypt, where at last she was delivered by the divine touch and the inbreathing of the spirit of the god. From her deliverance they draw hope, and as her kindred they appeal, first to the gods, then to the Argive King. There is no lack of excitement. Entreaties, flatteries, reproaches, culminate in threats of suicide. When the minions of their persecutors drag the shrieking maidens from the altars, only to be stopped in the nick of time by the arrival of the King, no one will call the situation undramatic. But the Chorus, not the actors, make it vivid. Old moralizing Danaus (a dim ancestor of Polonius) and good scrupulous King Pelasgus are mere foils to the energy and pathos, the fanaticism and barbaric charm of the Danaids. The two actors are present: the tool is invented: but the poet makes little use of it.

Lyrically the work is a masterpiece. The poet's imaginative power is already revealed. He sees the suffering and struggles of the maidens as an image of the way in which, to some strange end, God seems to guide the world. 'The paths of his secret purpose wind,' they say, 'in tangled gloomy thickets, dark beyond discerning.' Yet 'the President of the

Immortals' has a Plan. He hurls ambitious mortals to destruction, and sits above, immovable, untiring, working out 'his effortless Harmony' according to his Will. That strain had not been heard in European poetry before. It has been echoed often. Drummond of Hawthornden remembered it when he wrote, 'Beneath a sable veil and shadows dim . . the World's great Mind His secret hid doth keep.' It is the source of Hardy's 'Immanent Will,' working 'eternal artistries in Circumstance.'[4]

Can men unravel the maze? The poet does not say so. But there are hints of laws to guide us. In the lost sequel the Danaids were forced into the marriage. Their father bade them kill their husbands. One, Hypermestra, disobeyed. She was destined to become the mother of a race of heroes. Aphrodite vindicated her in a speech from which some lines survive:

Pure Heaven is moved with yearning for the Earth,
And Earth grows passionate for her Lord's embrace:
Rain falls from the parent Sky, whereby the Earth
Is moistened and conceives. From that bright shower
Whereof I also am the cause, are sprung
Demeter's corn, the cattle of the field,
And fruits of all the seasons, for man's use.[5]

Hypermestra, cleaving to her husband, fulfils nature's law. Human love and suffering are part of nature's travail. It is a reinterpretation of the primitive religious notion that all things are born from Mother Earth and the Sky Father. Anaxagoras, Euripides, Lucretius link it again with their own philosophies. Marcus Aurelius finds comfort in it, when he writes: 'Whatever the Nature of the Universe brings to each man is for his good. . . The Earth desires the rain with love, and with love the holy Aether desires: the Universe with love desires to create whatever is to be born.' Modern echoes are innumerable.

Aeschylus fought at Marathon and Salamis. He saw the burning of the Athenian shrines by Xerxes, and his *Persae* (472 B.C.) interprets the Greek victory as the work of Nemesis. The extent and luxury of the Persian Empire and the veneration which its monarchs claimed, seemed to Greek eyes a provocation of the gods. That view he shares. In this play there are even traces of the notion which he later repudiated, that the gods are jealous of all greatness and tempt men wantonly to ruin. It is easy to accept such doctrine about enemies.

But the thought that arrogance sows crime and reaps death as the harvest is applied impartially to Greeks and Persians. In sober earnestness he reads the great deliverance as a proof of justice in an ordered universe.

He lays his scene in Persia, and imagines the reception of the news by the court. The lyrical introduction, which describes the dazzling and apparently irresistible splendour of the Persian host, has an undercurrent of foreboding. It creates an atmosphere for the arrival of the Queen-Mother Atossa. That is a new and promising use of lyric. Atossa is the embodiment of pride in Xerxes and of haunting fear for him.

A Messenger brings news of the defeat. Atossa listens silently to his disordered cries and to the wailing of the Persians. At last she speaks: 'I have been silent long. Calamity has made me dumb. . . Who has not fallen?' The Messenger reads her mind. 'Xerxes,' he says, 'is among the living. He beholds the light of day.' 'A light indeed to me. . .'[6]

This Queen, so still among the agitated Persians, is the first of many silent heroines. A fantastic scene of oriental magic follows. Darius is evoked to prophesy fresh evil, and to warn his people against arrogance. It is the first, and not the least impressive ghost-scene of our tragic stage. But Xerxes, when he appears, is a weak creature, a nonentity who has ruined a great heritage, not a tragic hero.

The first tragic hero that we know is Eteocles, in the *Seven against Thebes* (467 B.C.). This young prince, who is organizing the defence of Thebes, has courage, eloquence and generosity. But his life is shadowed by a curse, invoked on him and on his brother by their father, Oedipus. 'They shall divide their heritage with the sword.' He sees the curse in process of fulfilment. The Argives are fighting to dethrone him, and to seat his brother on the throne. His preparations for defence are interrupted by a mob of panic-stricken women. He saves the situation by his energy. But he betrays the rashness in his character which will ruin him in the end. A Messenger describes the Argive champions, and the King despatches a Theban leader against each. Finally, he learns that his brother is challenging him to mortal combat. It rests with him to accept or to refuse. The Chorus beg him to control himself and send another champion. Instead of that, in a spirit of fatalism, stung by his brother's insults, and moved by an heroic, but mistaken sense of honour, he goes himself. The curse is fulfilled. The son of Oedipus kills his brother and is killed by him.

What, we may ask, has become of our boasted 'justice in an ordered universe?' Why should Eteocles suffer for the folly of his ancestors? Aeschylus neither ignores nor answers the question. His hero is a member of a tainted family, haunted by his father's curse, as by a living, malignant influence. But at the crisis there is an act of his own will, a conscious choice of evil. We do not know why Zeus permits us to be faced by odds so desperate: why, in fact, the dice are loaded. But good and evil, it appears, are not quite capriciously distributed, like the gifts from the two jars in the *Iliad*. 'Fie on these mortals!', said Zeus, in the *Odyssey,* 'they blame the gods, yet they themselves are also to blame.'[7] Eteocles is a full-grown tragic hero, the victim partly of circumstance, partly of his own character and choice.

One of the guesses made by Aeschylus at the solution of life's moral tangle was that suffering is God's discipline for men:

> Zeus, whosoe'er He be . . hath set men's feet in the way of Wisdom, and ordained as Law, having authority, ' By Suffering, Knowledge.' As in sleep the old wound wakes, the pain of conscience trickles at the heart, and then, against men's will, Discretion comes, a grace, I think, forced on them violently by Spirits seated on the awful bench.[8]

The thought, developed by Plato and combined with Hebrew ideas, has become a commonplace. In the *Prometheus,* Aeschylus suggests that even Zeus had to learn his lesson once. Far from leading us at first in paths of wisdom, he wanted to destroy us. His second, subtler plan, was to keep us ignorant and therefore harmless. Prometheus, the spirit of intelligent Forethought, as our friend, stole us a portion of the sacred fire from heaven, and instructed us in arts that make life tolerable. For the theft he was punished. Zeus tortured, but could not kill him. For, like Zeus, he is immortal. In the end Zeus had to learn that he could not rule by violence alone without the help of wisdom. And Prometheus had to make a compromise with strength.

Chained and rivetted with adamantine nails to the cliffs of Scythia, the hero is silent while the ministers of Zeus, the craftsman-god Hephaestus, and Brute-Strength and Violence, do their work. Alone at last, he breaks the silence with a cry:

> Bright air of heaven, swift-winged winds, and river-springs; innumerable laughter of the ocean-waves, and thou, All-Mother, Earth . . see what I suffer, a god by gods afflicted.[9]

His cry and the noise of rivetting have been heard in the sea-caves and pools below. There is a stir of wings, and he is visited by Nymphs, fair shapes in which Greek fancy embodied the mists that rise from waters and hover on the mountain-side. They cannot help, but their pity touches him and he relates his story. Their father Ocean follows, riding a marvellous winged monster. He is all discretion, and he offers mediation. Prometheus will not hear of it, and we exult, though the Nymphs and Ocean grieve. A new strain in the lyrics quickens our sense that the whole human race is sympathizing with its champion, and Io, a representative of suffering humanity, appears. She is a victim, like Prometheus, of the tyranny of Zeus; but she is also, as we know from the *Suppliants,* a symbol of the mystery by which, through love and suffering, nature brings life to birth. Prometheus pities her, wins her confidence, and prophesies her trials and deliverance. In Egypt she will be restored, and will bear a son. From her race will spring a son of Zeus who will also be a labourer for man, Heracles, destiny's conciliator in the Titan's quarrel. In him Prometheus will recognize 'the dear son of a hated father,' and by his help Prometheus will be freed and reconciled with Zeus.

For the present we rejoice in his defiance. The scene culminates in his revelation that the power of Zeus is not absolute. The day will come when, if Zeus follows his own impulse, he will beget a son more powerful than himself, and be overthrown. Prometheus knows the secret. Zeus must perish, or approach him humbly as a suppliant for knowledge.

The boast is overheard, and Hermes comes from Zeus to demand an explanation. Prometheus answers with contempt. Neither threats from Hermes nor pleading from the Nymphs can move him. With a final warning, Hermes goes. In the thunder of a gathering storm, the Nymphs decide to share the hero's destiny. The mountains open, and the Titan, with the Nymphs, whose love has triumphed over fear, is engulfed in Tartarus.

The sequel is lost. After an age of suffering, Prometheus was brought back to the upper air, still bound. A vulture came to him daily, and devoured his flesh. He was visited by his brother Titans, once prisoner like him, now free, and by Heracles, whom he advised about his travel in the west, as, in our play, he had prophesied to Io her adventures in the east. Heracles shot the vulture, and Zeus assented to the liberation of Prometheus and his worship as a benefactor of man. The Trilogy ended with the inauguration of his cult at Athens.

There remains the *Oresteia* (458 B.C.), the greatest work of Aeschylus, if not, as Swinburne [10] said, of man; a dramatic symphony — the word is suitable, for the form is musical — in three movements. The first is concerned with Clytaemnestra's murder of her husband, its motives and its effect on her; the second with the vengeance taken by her son, Orestes, its motives and the effect on him; the third with the great issues raised by these events, as viewed not merely by the actors, but by society and the gods. The three movements are vitally connected, and the contrasted themes, which are stated in the first, are developed in the second and third with increasing tragic discord, till at last they are resolved in a magnificent harmony at the end. Each movement has its own dramatic scheme, built up on simple musical designs, which anyone familiar with our own sonata form can readily apprehend. The form, far from diminishing the intensity of the action, is the means by which the artist has endowed his characters with almost superhuman energy.

Before the play began, the audience knew the outline of the story. But on several important questions they did not know what view the dramatist would take. For instance, what was Clytaemnestra's motive? Love of Aegisthus, or revenge for Iphigeneia? Or both? If it was vengeance, was it justified? Was Agamemnon right in sacrificing his daughter? Or was the prophet who demanded it mistaken, and Agamemnon a criminal? Again, was Orestes, as some versions held, a hero, justly avenging a monstrous outrage? Or, as the authorities at Delphi would suggest, a reluctant, righteous minister of Apollo, saved from the Furies and exonerated by the god? Or a criminal in whose favour there were mitigating circumstances, justly tormented by the Furies, but mercifully released by an Athenian verdict through the intervention of Athena? By his sincere and original answers to these questions, Aeschylus has profoundly influenced our own religious and political ideas. But his first, sufficient purpose was the creation of a noble work of art.

The play begins. A watchman, posted on the palace-roof at Argos, speaks. His first words tell us that it is a starry night. After a year of anxious watching, he is still hoping against hope for the beacon-signal which will mean that Troy has fallen. But by the form of this first speech Aeschylus has contrived to give us our first sense of the mysterious gloom which hangs over the city, and of its cause — the Queen, her half-suspected disloyalty, and her unknown, unsuspected, but no less real determination to avenge her child.

For a whole year of watching I have prayed the Gods for Deliverance from these Troubles — this palace-roof of the Atreidae my only bed through all these nights; till I have learnt to know by heart the general assembly of the stars, and those particular bright potentates that bring men storm and summer, the constellations, brilliant in the aether, their rising and their setting: and I am watching still for the sign of a light, a gleam of fire, bringing from Troy a message, news of capture, because I must obey my orders from a masterful, sanguine, man-willed Woman.

When I pass my nights here, tramping my anxious beat on the dew-drenched roof, my only bed — unvisited by dreams — no dreams for me — fear at my side, not sleep, but fear of the sleep from which one would be sure of never waking —

Well, when I think to sing or hum a tune, mixing myself, as it were, a dose of music, to comfort me instead of sleep, I weep for the misfortune of this House, not governed well, as it used to be.

But now, I pray the Gods for Deliverance from Trouble with the shining of the fire by night.[11]

If we examine this passage with the analogy of the sonata form in our minds, we shall be able to appreciate the later developments of the poem. Here we have, to begin with, the simple form: 'I pray for Deliverance: transition: the Woman: transition: I pray for Deliverance.'

As if in answer to the prayer, the Watchman sees, and makes us see in imagination, the beacon flaring on the hills.

All hail! O Light, bringing dayspring in the night, news to make Argos dance and sing for joy.

Ho there! I call to Agamemnon's Wife to rise and

sing a Hallelujah for the fall of Troy, the news this beacon brings us!

I myself will be the first to dance, because this Light brings me, as well as my good master, good luck.[12]

Once more, the form is both musical and dramatic. Light and Dances: Agamemnon's Wife: Dances and Light. The masterful man-willed Woman was at the centre of the first dramatic paragraph. Agamemnon's Wife dominates the second.

He dances, but something checks him. He speaks for the third time, then goes.

Well, well — I pray I may welcome my master home, and clasp his hand in loving greeting. For the rest I am silent. . . The House, if it could find a voice, would tell a plain tale. As for me, to those who know, I speak freely: to others — I forget.[13]

From within a woman's voice is heard, crying 'Hallelujah.' We know it is Clytaemnestra, rejoicing, not for her husband's safety, but for her day of vengeance.

After the cry, silence. Then a company of old men gather before the palace, ignorant of what has happened, anxious to know. The rhythm changes from iambic (blank verse) to a solemn march, as they move, half-chanting, half-muttering their thoughts.

Ten years have passed since Priam's great antagonist, King Agamemnon, and his brother Menelaus, Zeus-dowered princes, launched their armies against Troy.

With a cry — the War-god's cry — they went, like vultures, robbed of their young, screaming for vengeance: 'circling on wings that beat like beating oarblades, they cry in desolate grief for their high-nested children: they have lost the labour for their young that kept them faithful, guarding the nest.'

Some god in the height, Pan, or perhaps Apollo, or Zeus, hears the cry, and soon or late sends on the sinner's head an avenging Fury.

(*Enter* Clytaemnestra *from the Palace. She pours drink-offerings and burns incense at the altar, silently. The old men do not see her yet.*)

So Zeus sent the sons of Atreus against Paris: it was His intent to lay on Greeks as well as Trojans a burden of war and grief in that quarrel for an adulterous woman.

The matter is as now it is, and it must end where Fate appoints. By no burnt sacrifice, by no outpouring of an unburnt offering, can the sinner charm the stubborn wrath of Zeus.

We are old and frail. We could not go to war. Weak infancy and old age are alike in that: no strength for fighting. We are like withered, sapless trees; like dreams abroad in daylight. (*They see the Queen.*)

But thou, daughter of Tyndareus, Queen Clytaemnestra, what is the meaning of these sacrifices? Have you some news? Why are the altars of the gods throughout the city, the gods of heaven, the gods of the nether world, ablaze with gifts, columns of fire, now here, now there, mounting to heaven, drugged by the innocent Persuasion of royal unguent? Tell us, if you can, if it be right to tell; and heal this anxious, heart-devouring care, to which the sight of sacrifices seems to bring some gleam of hope.[14]

She does not answer, but departs, in religious silence, as if to worship at the other altars of the city. As they wait for her return, they break into full song, in a flowing epic rhythm, which is modified and superseded by more solemn and more complex metrical patterns as the song develops. They are still haunted by memories and fears.

When the two Kings went forth, there came an omen, two eagles, feasting on a pregnant hare. The prophet read it as a sign that the Kings would conquer. But Artemis, he said, was angry with the eagles, and might demand some dreadful sacrifice in retribution.

Amid such memories, we have no comfort save the thought of Zeus, and of His law ' By Suffering, Knowledge.'

The prophet had his will. When the fleet was detained by adverse winds at Aulis, he clamoured for the sacrifice of Iphigeneia. The King — ' criticizing no prophet ' — after irresolute murmuring, steeled himself to the wicked deed, ' emboldened by the wretch Temptation, child of designing Ruin.' He yielded. He bade them take his child —

' She stood, with her saffron veil falling about her, looking for pity to her sacrificers, showing as in a picture, wishing to speak to them, as often in her father's hall, lovingly, in pure and perfect maidenhood, she had sung for her dear father the happy hymn that graced the third drink-offering — to Zeus the Saviour — at his feast. What followed I did not see, nor do I tell. Only, the design of Calchas was not without fulfilment. May the end be good . . as is the wish of this, the nearest, closest to the throne. . .' [15]

It is Clytaemnestra, who has returned. And now she speaks. Her tragic motherhood dictates the phrase in which she tells them of her husband's triumph:

> With good news, as the proverb runs, may Morning come to birth from her Mother, Night. You are to learn a joy surpassing hope. The Greeks have taken Troy.

After short sentences of her contempt for the dazed, incredulous, but happy Chorus, the note recurs. 'Troy fell,' she says, 'within the Night, I tell you, that has brought this Day to birth.'[16]

'What messenger could come so quickly?' 'The God of Fire. He kindled a beacon-light on Ida, and watchmen flashed it on from peak to peak until at last, it swooped from the Spider's crag, near home, on the palace of the sons of Atreus, this light, whose ancestor was the fire at Troy. Such is the manner of my torch-racers, the last who runs no less a victor than the first. My husband sent me the news from Troy.'

'Tell us the tale again!' 'The fall of Troy? There are cries of triumph and despair, blending not well. Pour oil and vinegar in the same flask, you will say they are enemies, not friends. What of the vanquished? They are falling on the bodies of their dear ones, dead — and they not even free to weep their fill. The victors will be happy, off guard. They should be cautious. Will they refrain from outrage? If so, all may be well. The hate of the dead may not pursue them, unless they sin, or unless some unexpected evil happen. . . I speak as an anxious woman. May the good prevail.' (*Exit* Clytaemnestra.)

Zeus has vindicated his authority, sing the Chorus. Paris sinned: Troy fell. Ruin threw her net about the towers, and Zeus struck his blow. The fool hath said: ' God takes no heed of mortals when they trample under foot the loveliness of holy things.' This manifest judgment refutes him. Temptation came to Paris. Like a boy chasing a bird, he chased the bright Illusion. Death was the dowry Helen took with her to Troy.

At home, she left the noise of warlike preparation, and the silence of a desolate house, and a husband, shamed but unreviling, dreaming of her still. When he seems to see his happiness, the vision, in that instant, slips from his arms and is gone, on wings that travel down the roads of sleep. These are the sorrows of the royal house, and worse than these. Nay, in every home is heard the cry of the breaking heart for the men who went from Greece.

Beautiful men went out, and the War-God, like a money-changer who takes masses of base metal and gives in exchange a little precious gold, took their bodies, and sent home a little heap of ashes in an urn. They praise their dead, and they mutter curses on the war-makers.[17]

May not the gods be angry too? My heart waits anxiously for news still cloaked in Night. God doth take heed of sinners who have blood on their hands. A man who prospers without righteousness sooner or later finds fortune changed. The Furies make him pine and dwindle. Then, when he is lost in darkness, there is no more hope.

The King is coming. Enter a veteran, who heralds his approach. Why such depression, he asks? A soldier has more cause for gloom than civilians. Think of the hardships of campaign, the sleepless nights, the cold 'that killed the birds,' the intolerable heat 'when the sea sank in his windless bed at noon, waveless, asleep.' Think of the dead, asleep. 'They do not even care to rise again.' Banish gloom, and sing of the greatness of King Agamemnon, the conqueror, the greatest man on earth!

The Queen has entered. She will not listen

to the Herald. ' My husband will tell me everything. Bid him come quickly, and find his wife as he left her, faithful, no seal broken in his time of absence. I have no more knowledge of pleasure or reproach from any other man than I have skill to dip and temper sword-blades.'

She goes, and the Elders turn to what they think will be a happier theme. What of Menelaus? Is he with the King? No, he is lost in a storm, probably shipwrecked; not a fit topic for a day of rejoicing.

The Elders brood again on Helen, charming, fatal temptress. She was like a young lion-cub, a delightful playmate, fawning bright-eyed for food, but at last revealed in its true nature as a priest of Ruin. Such was Helen, smiling, flattering, beautiful, but, in the end, a bride of tears, a Fury.

Clytaemnestra, Helen's sister, stands before the palace, waiting for Agamemnon.

Agamemnon arrives. He talks of God and Justice, phrasing his gratitude for great work which he and God have done. Tomorrow he will look into affairs of state. Today is sacred to religion. Clytaemnestra listens. He ignores her.

She speaks, but not at first to him. ‘Elders of Argos, I will not blush to show you how I love this man. Time wears modesty away. The story I shall tell is my own, my life when he was at Troy. It is a bad thing for a woman to sit husbandless, alone, and hear the cruel messengers, one hot on another's heels, each with worse news. Had this man been wounded as often as rumour said, he would have been more full of holes than a net. If he had died as often as he was reported dead, he might have been a triple-bodied monster, dying once for every body. Such cruel rumours have even made me lay hands on myself, and others have loosed me from the rope.’

She turns to her husband. It is an anxious moment. ‘Orestes is not here to meet you. I sent him to a friend for safety. I feared there might be mischief brewing in your absence. . .’ She grows bolder. ‘The fountains of my tears are dry: not a drop left. My eyes are worn out with watching for you, waiting for you, the lover's lamp still burning for you, though the lover came not.’ She heaps phrase on phrase of adulation, then she tempts him. ‘Nay, my lord, set not on the ground the foot which trampled Troy. Women, why are you slow? You know your task, to strew his way with tapestries. Instantly let his road be strewn with purple, that Justice lead him to a home scarce hoped for.'

For a moment he resists. If he treads the purple, he assumes the attributes of a god. Devilishly she pursues what seems a flattering whim. Would not Priam have accepted god-like honours? Is Agamemnon less than Priam, or a coward, afraid of the mob? Will he not show his strength, by yielding a little victory to a weak woman? He thinks she loves him, and he yields. But he insults her in the same moment. 'Be kind to this woman, a choice Trojan captive.' It is Cassandra, whom he has brought with him as his concubine. Clytaemnestra ignores her for the present. She is busy chanting her terrible triumph-cry as the King treads the purple road to the net of Ruin.

She returns, amid the muttering of the confused and anxious Chorus. 'You too, Cassandra, come in.' Her brutality to the slave revolts us, and the leader of the Chorus touches the heart of the tragedy when he says, 'But I, because I pity, will not be angry.'

Clytaemnestra goes, and Cassandra moves towards the palace, then recoils. In vision after vision, she sees it as a charnel-house, haunted by shapes of murdered children, by a choir of Furies, dancing on the roof and singing of blood and hate. She sees the Queen's plot, the bridal-bath of welcome, the purple net of broidery in which she traps and kills her husband. Last of all, she sees herself, as a second victim. Strangely and beautifully, she grows calmer. She tries to warn the old men, but they cannot understand. She finds plain words, but they are shocked, incredulous. She gives up her effort. A vision of Apollo and a premonition of the just avenger come to her, as she renounces her prophetic office. She passes to death with gentle thoughts of Priam and her brothers, and with a cry of pity for all suffering humanity. 'Alas, for mortal life. In prosperity, it shows but as a sketch, a shadow. In adversity, as a picture wiped out at a touch by a wet sponge. I pity that more than the other.'[18]

As the prayer for Deliverance from Trouble was the keynote of the prelude, and Justice the repeated catchword of the duel between Agamemnon and his wife, so Pity is the first note and the last of Cassandra's scene. Pity as well as fear are in our hearts when we wait and listen for the cry which we know is coming from the palace. It comes. It is Agamemnon's voice. 'Alas, I am hit! A mortal blow! ' and again, 'Alas, again, ah me! a second blow!'

The old men hesitate and argue for a few tense moments, then nerve themselves to break in. But the doors fly open, and Clytaemnestra stands before us, triumphant over the bodies of her victims.

I will not blush to say the opposite of many things I said before to suit the time. How could one fence high, unescapable, the net of Ruin by avowing open hate to enemies, thought friends? I pondered long on this struggle, the crisis of an old dispute. At last, at last, it came. I stand where I struck, over the deed done. I so contrived — I will not deny it — that he should not escape or guard himself. I twined an endless coil about him, like a net for fishes, an opulent robe of death, and struck him twice. So he slacked his limbs. But I, as he lay there, gave him yet a third blow — for grace to Hades, the only Saviour of the dead. He splashed me with his blood, and I rejoiced, like the young corn in the bright rain of heaven at the time of the birth-travail of the bud. Blood were the only fit libation to be poured over this body. The cup of evil that he filled to overflowing, he has drunk himself to the dregs, and he is gone.[19]

From hysterical triumph, she passes to grim statement of the fact: 'This is my husband, Agamemnon, killed by my hand's just workmanship'; then to self-defence, 'Did he not kill my child?'; then to threats, in answer to the threatening Chorus. She names Aegisthus, and in the same breath cries against the faithlessness of Agamemnon. She reviles Cassandra. Her frightful energy dominates the Chorus, but her soul is in agony. She sees herself as an Incarnation of the vengeful Fiend, which haunts the house, fed fat on mischief, claiming his toll of blood from every generation. At last, when the broken Elders wail hopelessly, 'Who shall bury him?' she cries 'Not you! Not you! We struck him down, and down we will bury him, with no lamenting from his household. Iphigeneia, his daughter, lovingly, as is fitting, shall meet her father at the swift straits of sorrow, and shall throw her arms about him, and shall kiss him.'[20] She is thinking of a scene at Aulis, when the unsuspicious child broke from her mother's arms and ran to kiss her father. She is tragically tired. She longs for peace. She will make a bargain with the Fiend, and gladly live a life of simple poverty, if only, with this act of hers, 'the long madness of mutual killing' can be finished.

It is impossible. Her lover appears. A vulgar bully, revelling in his triumph, he rouses the Chorus, cowed and shaken by the Queen, to fresh resistance. 'Orestes!' they cry, and at the name Aegisthus calls his bodyguard. Clytaemnestra has been listening in silence to his ranting. Now she intervenes. 'No, no, my friend, let us do no more wrong.' At least she will prevent more bloodshed. She dismisses the Elders, and draws Aegisthus with her into the Palace. 'You and I, together, masters of this house, will order all things well.'

Years have passed, and night broods again over the Palace. Orestes prays for vengeance at his father's grave. Again the prayer is answered with a kindling of lights, a woman's cry, and a ritual of drink-offerings. But the cry is Clytaemnestra's shriek of terror, and the lights are kindled at her order when she wakes from an appalling dream. The offerings are the vain propitiation which she bids Electra, the King's persecuted daughter, to offer on her behalf at her husband's grave. At the suggestion of the Chorus, savage Trojan captive-women, Electra prays, not for her mother, but for her brother and herself, and for the coming of an avenger. Orestes reveals himself, and a tremendous ritual of incantation follows. The dead man's spirit is roused. At the beginning, Electra is a gentle child, and Orestes a young, buoyant soldier, enlisted in a brave cause, ignorant of life and war. Before the end, Electra has grown hard, and Orestes is transformed into a ruthless instrument of vengeance. The dead man's spirit has possessed him. When he meets his mother he will be implacable.

They meet, and Orestes tells her the false news of his own death, to gain admission to the Palace. Her cry, though it is quickly smothered, shows that she has remained a mother, hoping that somehow Orestes might be spared, but harmless. When she hears he is dead, she cries out, with a sense of utter loneliness, against the curse which robs her so persistently of all she loves. The moment passes. She bullies Electra, and welcomes the supposed messengers into the house. Then instinctively she feels suspicious. She sends for Aegisthus, choosing by a strange irony the old nurse of

Orestes as her messenger. Let Aegisthus come at once, with his guard.

A cry is heard within, and the Chorus think the vengeance has begun. It is the Nurse, lamenting her darling's death. She remembers him as a baby, and her homely, babbling reminiscences touch us, just before he takes his vengeance, with the thought that he is a son of woman, once a helpless infant, crying for the breast. Once more the poet has taken care to fill our hearts with human pity just before the crisis. The Chorus give the nurse a hint of comfort, and bid her tell Aegisthus not to bring his guard.

Aegisthus walks into the trap, and we hear his death-cry. A terrified servant shouts for Clytaemnestra. She appears. Her first impulse is to fight. She calls for 'a man-slaying axe' — with that weapon she killed Agamemnon. Then she realizes. Orestes stands pointing at the dead body of her lover. She is a mother again, pleading for mercy. She bares her breast, and for the first time he realizes. She is his mother. What can he do? The voice of Pylades reminds him of Apollo's strict command. The moment passes. He is hard again. She moves into the Palace, and he follows.

We wait, but there is no cry within. We know that the son is killing his mother, while the vindictive Trojan women shout a triumphant Hallelujah — the same cry with which the Trilogy began. With this act of vengeance, they assert, the house is cleansed, and 'the light has come.'

In fact the net of Ruin has claimed another victim. Standing where Clytaemnestra stood to justify her vengeance, Orestes spreads the fatal robe as evidence of her guilt. As he speaks, his reason is clouded. He becomes his own accuser, and at last, though no one else can see them, he sees the Furies, and rushes, mad, from the scene.

The first movement began with the Watchman's prayer for Deliverance from Trouble, the second with Orestes' prayer for vengeance. The third begins with the gentle, reconciling prayer of Apollo's priestess at Delphi to the gods of earth and heaven. She passes into the temple, and we hear her startled cry: she has seen the Furies in the shrine: it thrills us, as we were thrilled before by Clytaemnestra's Hallelujah and by Clytaemnestra's shriek of conscience-stricken fear. In the *Agamemnon,* Clytaemnestra poured her libations, and we knew she prayed for vengeance: then, in her triumph, she cried that blood was the only fit libation for the body of her husband. In the *Libation-Bearers* that grim taunt has been terribly fulfilled. She sent her drink-offerings to the grave, but they were used against her; and in the end, her son shed her blood as the only possible propitiation. Now, in his turn he is claimed by the Furies, the representatives of his mother's right to Justice. Must it go on for ever, blood always calling for blood? The religion of Delphi says: 'No. Orestes acted as the servant of Apollo. The mother's blood must indeed be expiated, but the god, who is responsible for the act of vengeance, can grant his servant absolution — not until he has suffered, nor until he has been purified by the god himself with the blood of a sacrificial victim.' So the third libation is the ceremonial cleansing of Orestes by Apollo.

But for Aeschylus, as an Athenian, the Delphic explanation is not adequate. Apollo may lull the Furies to sleep for a time; he may drive them from his temple with contumely; but they must still pursue their victim. Apollo's sanction cannot justify, Apollo's cleansing cannot atone.

So Clytaemnestra's spirit, tortured and implacable, wakes the Furies —

'I, Clytaemnestra, am the voice that calls, the dream that wakes you.' It is the climax of her tragedy. The Furies are henceforth the incarnation of her spirit. They track their victim to Athens, to the shrine of a goddess wiser, greater than Apollo. In the song with which they bind him as their own, the theme of the net of Ruin reaches its culmination:

Sing we the spell, Sisters of Hell;
Chant we the charm, mighty to harm,
Binding the blood, madding the mood. . .[21]

As Orestes falls, he breathes Athena's name. The bright goddess, in whose name Athens is to kindle a new hope in the world, appears. She listens to the pleas. A husband's murder could not go unpunished. A mother's blood cries out for expiation. She will not judge the issue, but refer it to a company of her citizens, the first, most venerable court of human justice. They hear the case. Their votes are equal. Human justice fails. What remains?

Athena has declared that, if the votes prove equal, she herself will vote for mercy. Orestes must go free. Blessing his deliverer, he goes.

But the Furies are not satisfied. They claim justice without compromise. They threaten to destroy the city which has wronged them. Graciously, not by force, but by divine Persuasion, Athena charms them from their purpose. They shall have an honourable place as guardians of ordered justice in a civilized community. The old rule of vengeance must be merged in a new rule of law and mercy. So Athena stands, to justify her cause, not to Argive Elders or Trojan slaves, but to the Furies. She prevails, and, for the Hallelujah of vengeance, the robe of Ruin, the lights which kindled with false promise and the drink-offerings of blood, we have the Hallelujah of peace, the torches and drink-offerings of Athena's festival, and the scarlet robes with which her handmaidens invest the Kindly Goddesses, once known as Furies.[22]

There are details in the religious symbolism which ring false to us — Athena's theological reason for her vote, Apollo's fantastic biology. What matters is the main conclusion. For nations, not for individuals only, the substitution through intelligence of ordered law for the red rule of vengeance is the only hope of suffering humanity.

II. THE WORK OF SOPHOCLES

SOPHOCLES (496–406 B.C.) is said to have been chosen for beauty and musical skill to lead a procession of Athenian boys at the celebration of Salamis. He was a friend of Pericles, and several times held office in the state. His dramatic success began before the death of Aeschylus and continued to the end of a long life. In the prime of his manhood Athens was mistress of the Aegean, and seemed to her lovers to have solved, so far as human wit can solve it, the problem of good government. In the *Oresteia* Aeschylus extolled her as a home of ordered justice, a high achievement of intelligence and a symbol of the harmony which he divined beyond the stress and chaos of men's tragic struggles. Pericles, in the Funeral Oration, sees the achievement as a work of compromise, of balance, the discovery of a golden mean. Athenians, he claims, are equal before the law, yet rewarded in degree according to excellence. They love beauty without sacrificing simplicity, and pursue wisdom without loss of strength. Not less valiant than the products of the Spartan barrack, nor less open-minded than the Ionians to whom they offer hospitality, they believe that action is not paralyzed by thought, nor freedom inconsistent with respect for law.[23]

The buoyancy and the sense of equilibrium, which mark the years between the rise of Pericles and the beginning of the Peloponnesian war, are reflected in the Parthenon, the art of Pheidias and the plays of Sophocles. His faith in the ideal of the great age seems hardly, if at all, affected by the scandals and tragedies of the war. He died a few months before the defeat of Athens, and was remembered after his death as one of those few mortals who may properly be called happy. 'For he lived a long life, made many beautiful tragedies, and, in the end, died without suffering any evil.'[24]

It is fashionable nowadays to contrast this traditional picture of Sophocles, as a successful citizen, a conscious artist, aiming at perfection in form, with a traditional Euripides, who broke the form for love of truth, and, for humanity's sake, endured unpopularity and exile. Surely, if Sophocles was so respectable, he cannot have been quite honest. If he was orthodox in accepting religious, social and political conventions which Euripides valiantly, and, in the long run, successfully exposed, must he not even have been stupid? Was he really content, amid the moral and material tragedy of Athens, to go on weaving perfect poetry? Surely there must have been in this great artist some lack of heart.

Nothing could be more unjust. His art retained its balance and clarity in the external chaos of the war because he had drawn strength to face external circumstance precisely from the ideal which made the age of Pericles so brilliant. That ideal of civilized life as a result of order, balance, moderation, was not proved futile because for the moment Athens failed. The equilibrium was not achieved without effort nor to be maintained without a struggle; and the men of the Periclean age were well aware of 'the unhappy accidents,' as Pericles calls them, to which all of us, and all human things are subject. They saw even the life of their beloved city as a kind of raft, constructed for good living in the midst of chaos. Their leader Pericles and their poet Sophocles knew that the raft was leaky, and that, by the terms on which human things exist, it might go to pieces. Birth and growth, decay and death are the conditions of mortality for institutions as for men and women. Still, the equilibrium achieved, the nobility of life attained, are at this moment worth while, no matter when or how the deluge comes.

'How marvellous is Man,' exclaim the Chorus in the *Antigone*.[25] He has invented ships and ploughs. He makes the beasts his servants. He has found out Speech, which gives wings to Thought, and he has learnt how to live in cities. Only, in spite of all his skill, Death and the Grave mock him. Yet the ordered life of cities and a spirit of reverence for law are great achievements.

So think the Theban citizens. They do not approve of Creon's edict, forbidding, under pain of death, the burial of Polyneices. But, when they hear it has been defied, their instinct puts them on its side. For men and cities alike, they say, respect for law is the one hope of safety. They disown the man whose disobedience imperils what human wisdom has contrived.

Their song is barely finished when Antigone is brought in by her accuser. Is it possible, they wonder, that she has been guilty of such folly? She admits it. She knew the edict. Creon himself is incredulous. How could she dare . . ?

> Because it was not Zeus who made this proclamation, nor has that Justice which dwells with the gods below prescribed such laws as this for the dealings of men with men. I did not think your edicts had such force that you, a mortal, could override the sure, unwritten ordinances of the gods.[26]

Athenians, said Pericles, respect the laws and the magistrates, but above all, ' those laws which are framed for the redress of injury, and those unwritten laws the breach of which is thought to be disgraceful.' Yes, but what if the written and the unwritten laws conflict? What if Athens, in a time of public danger, revived against a traitorous citizen the old Draconian Code, by which his body, under pain of death, must not be buried in Attic soil? What if Alcibiades, your nephew, had been the traitor, and Antigone had been your niece? Such issues, Sophocles knew, might arise not only in benighted, despot-ridden Thebes, but in democratic Athens under stress of war. And in fact they did arise, when Pericles was no longer alive to deal with them.

This play was produced in 441 B.C., and at that date, few Athenians would feel (as Hegel thought, and critics still repeat) that the clash was between right and right. Creon's edict is bad law, as based on the arbitrary *fiat* of a despot, and is a violation of the unwritten law which gives the dead their burial. And Creon, of all men, is the last who should ignore the claim. He holds his authority as next of kin to both the brothers. No, the clash is between bad law, enforced by a bigot, and the instinctive, loving devotion of a woman to her dead brother. In the first glow of exaltation after her heroic act she has no doubt. She knows the laws of God are on her side.

Presently Creon is asking: 'What of Eteocles? He was your brother too, and he died for Thebes. You dishonour him when you honour the man who wronged and killed him.' 'Who knows,' she falters, 'whether the dead esteem such things worth their care.' 'An enemy still hates his enemy even in the grave.' Is it so? She cannot tell. She can only answer: 'My nature is to join in loving, not in hating.' [2.7] That goes deeper even than the appeal to the unwritten law.

Unfortunately, bad laws, however bad, may

be backed with strength. Creon, enforcing his will, may or may not pull disaster on his own head and be taught his lesson. Before he learns it, he has power to give Antigone the choice of death or treason to her nature. The gods let her die, thinking at the end that her lover Haemon is on Creon's side, uncertain even of the gods, though not doubtful that she has chosen rightly. The gods have portents ready to warn Creon of his wickedness. Teiresias actually makes him see his error and attempt to set it right. He is too late to save Antigone, because he stops to right the wrong against Polyneices. Antigone has hanged herself. Haemon, his son, her lover, curses him, and kills himself. Eurydice, his wife, commits suicide. He is utterly broken. No doubt he was wrong. No doubt he is stupid, obstinate, odious. But if we ask Sophocles to explain why such things happen, we shall get no answer. It is a fine play: it is true to life. Is not that enough?

Sophocles holds that for mortals, modesty is the safest and most decent frame of mind. His gods will not abide our question. They destroy as well as bless. Their ways are not our ways, though they are guardians and in some sense vindicators of 'unwritten laws,' which, even if it means destruction, our highest instinct bids us obey. Reason bids us be modest in prosperity, and in adversity not over much cast down, respecting what we cannot understand. As Agamemnon said, and then forgot: 'the modest mind is the best gift of heaven.' [28] But there are men and women for whom circumstances or their character put the gift out of reach.

Ajax is the victim of his character. His father bade him fight and be victorious with heaven's aid. He answers that a good-for-nothing could win on such terms. He would do without the gods. Athena came to inspire him on the field. 'Stand by the others,' he cried; 'Where I fight, the line will hold.' Achilles fell, and Ajax claimed his armour, as the noblest living Greek. The chieftains gave it to Odysseus, their best counsellor. Ajax brooded on the humiliation, and conceived a mad design of wiping out the insult by murdering the chieftains. He went at night to do it. At the moment when he stood before Agamemnon's hut, Athena turned his rage to frenzy, so that he mistook a pack of huddling sheep and cattle for his enemies. He killed, as he imagined,

Agamemnon, Menelaus and others. Then he took prisoners, and drove them to his hut, among them a ram, which he supposed was Odysseus; this he fastened to the central pillar of the hut, for death by flogging.

The play begins in the last watch of this night. The outrage on the herds has been discovered. An eye-witness has reported that he has seen Ajax rushing madly, with a bloody sword, over the meadows. Odysseus, his personal enemy, but a man of eminently fair mind, investigates for himself the question whether or not the suspicion thus aroused is justified. He is examining the ground outside the hero's hut, and is baffled by the footprints. Athena watches him at the task. She congratulates him on the promptness with which, as usual, he has seized an opportunity against an enemy. 'Dear goddess, I hear your voice, and understand, even when you are far away, unseen. . . He is my enemy, as you say. . . He is accused of an outrage on our cattle, and I wish to know the truth.' 'I know. I have been watching. The report is true. But his intention was to murder the chiefs. He planned it, and he nearly succeeded.' 'What stopped him?' 'I did. I drove him mad. He thinks he has killed

Agamemnon. He imagines that the dumb beasts he is now torturing in the hut, are other Greek chiefs — including you. You shall see for yourself.'

After reading the *Oresteia,* we are jealous for the honour of Athena. At first sight we wonder whether Sophocles in this, his earliest surviving play, has not a little lowered the standard. Is it not, perhaps, a narrow, rather heartless orthodoxy, which represents Athena as 'vindictive'? What shall we then think of this goddess, who not only punishes Ajax for his arrogance, but makes a spectacle of him in his madness for her favourite, his enemy? Athena has her reasons, and her purpose is not vindictive, as we shall discover.

Odysseus shrinks: a madman's eyes are dangerous. 'What? Afraid? Was he not a brave good man before?' 'I should not have been afraid of him in his right senses.' She mocks his cowardice. She will not let the madman see him. Besides, 'what sweeter laughter is there than to laugh over a fallen enemy?' Twice she assures him that he is perfectly safe. Yet Odysseus still shrinks from the sight. She insists.

Ajax appears at her call, stark mad, boasting of his triumph, and of the torture reserved for

Odysseus. 'You see the might of the gods,' says Athena, when he has gone. 'Did you ever know a better man, or a man of sounder wits than this man used to be?' 'I pity him,' Odysseus answers, 'though he is my enemy . . having regard to my own lot, no less than his. For I see that we all are shadows.' Athena approves. One day, she says, can lay low and set up again all human things. It is absurd for men to boast of strength or riches. 'The gods love men of the safe, modest mind — and they hate the evil.' [29]

Through such pity and fear, according to Aristotle, Tragedy purges us. We are not gods and goddesses, but men and women. With Odysseus we do not hate the madman, but pity him, and tremble for ourselves. Athena loves Odysseus, because he understands.

But what of Ajax? Does she hate him? Is he one of the 'evil'? If that had been what Sophocles meant, he would have been bold indeed, and very far from orthodox. Ajax was a national hero, for whose honour Athenians were as jealous as for the honour of their goddess herself. Yet Sophocles has stated, as the basic assumption of his play, that Ajax, whether or not the Greek commanders wronged him, planned, and, but for Athena, would have executed their treacherous murder. He has stated it, not as a possible view, but as an indisputable fact, given us on the authority of Athena. She does not say: 'I drove him mad, and made him think of treachery'; on the contrary, she says: 'he planned the treachery, and would have killed the chiefs, had I not driven him mad.' As to his state of mind when he conceived his plan, she says nothing. We are to form our own impression. What we are not to do is to ride away with a vaguely comforting notion that Ajax was 'done to death by slanderous tongues,' and that the whole story of his treachery was trumped up by Odysseus. That version was current. Sophocles could have used it. He preferred to show that a man's a man for all that — even if 'all that' includes the worst that a man's enemies can truly say of him. Already, in the prologue, he has made us face the worst about him, and admire him.

His men, sailors from Salamis, are loyal souls, brave and happy when he prospers, bewildered, helpless, like 'frightened birds,' when he is — what? — 'either driven mad by some god, or else slandered by the Greeks.' Of course it must be slander. It must be Odysseus! 'Up, Ajax! We are nothing by ourselves, but your enemies have fled from your eyes ere now like noisy, startled birds. If you appear they may yet crouch silent, in terror of the mighty eagle.' But Tekmessa, his captive-wife, comes out and tells them 'the great, terrible, ruthless conqueror, Ajax' is laid low by madness. We catch the infection of this love. We too are all for Ajax. But we know they are wrong about Odysseus. We know the facts.

They tell Tekmessa, what she did not know, about the reported raid on the cattle. It fits in with what she can tell them and us, about Ajax. Clearly his mind was not normal when he went out in the night to kill; clearly he was mad when he came back. Obviously, he has not been slandered. But if he is mad, what savage god has done it? The Thracian War-God, or the Crimean Artemis, who loves human sacrifice? They little think it is a wiser, greater power than either. Ajax himself will tell them, it is Athena.

But, if Ajax has done this thing, they are all in danger. They are alarmed for themselves and him. Tekmessa loves him too well to think of that. She tells them he has now recovered reason. Oh, then things look better? No, worse, she says. When he was mad, we suffered; he was happy. Now we have to see him suffer too.[30]

He shouts within: 'Alas, woe is me!', then, 'Alas, my son, my son!' Then a cry for Teucer, his brother, the one man who might help — 'Where is Teucer? Will he go plundering for ever, while I perish?' Tekmessa opens the hut, and we see him, still agitated, but sane, among the shambles. He begs his men to kill him. He reviles himself. Tekmessa tries to check him. 'Away with you, get you gone!' he cries. No truce with sentiment here, no gentleness, or penitence. He curses his enemies, above all, Odysseus — if he could only kill them, then die himself. . . Ah, death is the solution. 'How can I look to gods or men for any good?' If he does not kill himself, the army will exact the price of treachery. He, Ajax, will be stoned to death. So he makes his resolve, 'Ye sea-ways, caves by the sea and pasture on the shore . . very long, very long, you have kept me here at Troy. But you shall not have me here any longer with the breath of life in me: let no sane man think it.' And after the resolve, he makes his affirmation: 'Streams of Scamander, ye are friendly to the Greeks: ye shall no longer see this man — I will speak proudly — this soldier on whose peer Troy has not looked in all the throng that came from Greece, though now I am thus laid low, without honour.' The words 'without honour' are the climax.[31]

Calmer now, his purpose clear (the rhythm reflects the change), he reviews the situation, justifies the decision. Tekmessa cannot move him. He has passed beyond her reach. 'Ajax,' the sailors venture, 'I wish you could pity her as I do. Then you would approve her words.' 'Approve? Why, I will praise her, if she is brave enough to do my bidding.' 'Dear Ajax, I will obey in everything.' 'Bring me my son.' Gravely, not unkindly, he approves her wisdom in keeping the boy away while he was dangerous. That is over. Lift him up. He will not shrink from the sight of blood, if he is his father's son. He is to be a soldier too, in a hard school. 'Be more fortunate, boy, than your father, but in all else, like him: then you will not be base. Meanwhile, in the happy ignorance of youth, grow, and be the joy of your mother's life.'[32] That, Ajax knows, will be Tekmessa's consolation. It is enough.

But the Greeks? Will they hurt the boy,

when his father has escaped them? Teucer must save him.

He bids his son farewell, and bequeaths him the shield, the symbol of his honour. Nothing remains except to vindicate that honour by death. Tekmessa intervenes again. 'By the gods, and for your child's sake, do not desert us. And think a little of me — it is a part of manly honour not to forget good we have received.' 'You give me too much pain. Do you not understand, I no longer owe the gods a debt of service.'

Tekmessa, I think, goes in with him, and when he reappears, with a drawn sword in hand, we realize both that his resolution is unchanged, and that his spirit has indeed been softened by her pleading, so that he feels it 'womanish,' no longer 'like tempered steel.' He pities her, and therefore has to deceive her. Besides, he needs solitude for his act. There must be no risk of intervention or failure. So he makes the speech in which he seems to yield. He will purify himself in the meadows by the sea. He will bury the sword. For the future he will bow to heaven and respect the sons of Atreus. 'They are rulers. They must have submission. All that is terrible and strong yields to authority. The weary round of night passes and lets the white-horsed day kindle her beams. The moaning sea is lulled to rest by the breath of the passing storm. Even all-conquering sleep looses what he has bound, and does not hold his prisoner for ever. Shall not we learn wisdom too?' He knows the philosophy of the modest mind well enough. But when he bids his wife 'go in and pray that what my heart desires may be accomplished' he is bidding her farewell.[33]

He goes, and the sailors break into a hymn of joy. They are interrupted by a Messenger with news that, for today, the hero must be guarded. His life is still in danger. Athena's wrath — the prophet Calchas says it — was due to his old arrogance, and will end today.

Ajax dies. The sword with which he kills himself was given him by Hector, his enemy. Now, he says, it proves his friend. He dies with a prayer that Teucer may defend his body, and with an imprecation of destruction on the whole Greek army. What are we to think?

Tekmessa finds the body first. The gods, she says, were his destroyers. His enemies have no cause to mock. He has what his heart desired.

Teucer comes, to defend the child, and give

Ajax burial, in spite of the Greeks. He says: 'I think the gods are the cause of this, as of all that happens. Let others think as they will.'

But Teucer, loyal and valiant as he is, does not hold the solution. The material power, and even the legal argument that traitors must be punished, remain with the weak blustering Menelaus, the cold, official Agamemnon. It is for Odysseus, the hero's enemy, to see the truth. He tells the King, not only human pity, but justice will be outraged if he treats this good and loyal soldier as a traitor. 'He was my enemy, but, though he hated me, I will say he was the best man I have seen of all the Greeks who came to Troy — except Achilles.' The gods themselves demand that such a man should have honour in the grave.

That is the answer to the question of the prologue — Was Ajax evil? Did Athena hate him? As for mortals 'it is not just to injure a good man after death, though it happen that you hate him.' Agamemnon is puzzled. 'Do you mean, you bid me let them bury him?' 'I do: for I myself shall die.'

Light breaks on Teucer as well. 'You are a good man, Odysseus.' But Odysseus must not have part in the burial. Ajax died unreconciled.

And Ajax is the hero. His son must lift his body, with Teucer. It is bleeding still. But Eurysakes is the son of Ajax. He will not shrink.

Ajax suffers as a result of his own character. Arrogance breeds delusion, sin and ruin. It is the Aeschylean cycle. But Athena, the goddess of reason, though she foils and breaks him, establishes his honour. Odysseus is her pupil.

No such comforting formula is suggested by the *Electra*. Here the heroine is by nature modest and religious. Circumstances thwart her instinct. It is not her fault. She cannot have 'the best gift of the gods' except at the price of what she thinks would be betrayal. No modification of an Aeschylean formula will explain her tragedy.

And yet, in breaking the Aeschylean mould, Sophocles pays a tribute to his predecessor. He builds his play on a hint from Aeschylus.

In the *Libation-Bearers*, when Clytaemnestra sends Electra with the offerings to Agamemnon's tomb, the child shrinks from her task. How can she pray for blessing from the father for the mother who killed him? The Trojan women are at hand to advise. 'Pray for Orestes.' Oh, gladly, she will do that. What else? 'Pray for vengeance on the murderers — pray for their death?' 'Can that be right? Is it religious?' 'Of course it is — to requite an enemy with evil.'

Electra obeys, but she was not born for hatred. She prays for blessing on herself, and for the home-coming of Orestes, then breathes her prayer for an avenger, 'putting the bad prayer,' as she says, 'in the middle of the good'; then prays again: 'Send blessing from below for us, thy children.' [34]

Orestes comes, and vengeance is taken. But the fruits are hate and desolation.

For herself, Electra prays: 'Give me a heart more modest and a hand more righteous than my mother's.' From that hint of a life's tragedy — it is only a hint, in Aeschylus — Sophocles creates his heroine. She is older than the Aeschylean Electra, old enough at the time of her father's murder to save her infant brother and give him to the keeping of the grim, but loyal servant, who rears him with the single thought of vengeance. She lives on, oppressed by the usurpers, loveless, except for the memory of Agamemnon and the hope of her brother's return. She sees her father's tomb insulted, and the day of the month on which he died commemorated by a festival. Her sister, Chrysothemis, bows to circumstances, hides her feelings, and is rewarded with a sort of kindness. Electra cannot compromise. She lives to keep a protest living, and her reward is persecution, hunger, hatred, even the threat of death. Orestes does not come, and she begins to faint under the burden. But in the name of righteousness she still protests. The price she pays is worse, in her own estimate, than loneliness or fear: it is the loss of decent modesty, the peculiar virtue of her sex. She makes a public spectacle of her grief: she is ashamed. 'I pray that if life bring me any good, I may not quietly enjoy it, if it means that I must check the wings of my shrill waiiing and leave my father dishonoured. If the dead man is to lie wretched, a negligible heap, and they are not to pay for it, there will be no more modesty or righteousness in the world.'[35] That is the paradox, the secret of her tragedy. For the vindication of righteousness and modesty she must be irreligious, shameless.

Orestes is totally unlike the Aeschylean hero. He is not the conscience-driven inheritor of an accumulated mass of wrong, goaded by threats from the dead and by the awful voice of Apollo. Educated by Agamemnon's servant in the simple faith that, when the time comes, he must vindicate his father's right, he does not question the morality of what appears a dangerous, but obvious duty. Apollo's sanction is not asked. It is assumed. The oracle is consulted only about the means of execution. That archaic view — the suggestion that it is the view of Sophocles is as ridiculous as it is revolting — is taken by the Argive women and by Electra. She never doubts that the vengeance is a religious duty: when she hears Orestes is dead, she thinks the duty devolves upon herself. But there is this difference between Orestes and Electra. He is by nature rather hard and unimaginative: she is sensitive, and is tortured by the consciousness that hatred of her mother, right and necessary as she thinks it, is an outrage. Orestes never meets Clytaemnestra till he goes into the house to kill her. Electra has lived with her: has told herself: 'I must be stern: I must forget she is my mother,' but has not forgotten it. Her mother's cruelty helps. It is easy to hate her when she celebrates her monstrous festival and reviles Orestes. When

Electra recounts these things to the Argive women, so wise, and so irrelevant with their talk of moderation, she cries again: 'I am ashamed . . but it is not possible, my friends, in such a life as mine to be modest and religious. Evil compels us to do evil.' [36]

When Chrysothemis pleads: 'Our father, I know, forgives,' Electra is stern and even cruel. But when she hears of the Queen's dream, the gleam of hope softens her. 'Dear sister, do not pollute the tomb with any of her gifts. . . Take a lock of your hair — and this of mine, alas, unkempt . . a small gift, but what I have. Pray for Orestes. . . I think—I think — some stirring of our father's spirit sent this dream. Anyhow, sister, do this for me, and for yourself, and for the dearest man in all the world, who lies in Hades, the father of us both.' [37] Electra can love, as well as hate.

Clytaemnestra is not penitent, but frightened and lonely. She wants to justify herself, even to Electra. Her plea is the sacrifice of her child. She spoils it by the savage argument that Menelaus, after all, and Helen had sons who might have been offered. Electra's answer 'It was lust, not vengeance' is conclusive. But Electra is blinded by her loyalty. Agamemnon killed his daughter, she admits, but for his country. Artemis demanded the sacrifice because, forsooth, Agamemnon as a child had offended her by boasting. The atmosphere of the play depends on this queer combination, in everyone, and most of all in the heroine, of savage superstition with capacity for the deepest human feeling. 'By what law,' she argues, 'can you justify your act, if I admit your motive was reprisal? Do you not see that if this law were valid, life for life, you would yourself in justice, be the first to die?'[38] Yet Electra is praying for Orestes to come home and act upon this law. Sophocles knew well enough that such revenge is worse than useless. It is part of Electra's tragedy that she does not know it. Even so, there comes the thought: 'This is my mother.' 'I am ashamed, be sure, even if I do not seem ashamed to you. I understand that what I do is out of measure, and does not befit me. Your enmity and your acts compel me.'[39]

Clytaemnestra prays to Apollo. Part of her prayer is silent, for Electra is listening. What is she praying for?

As if in answer, the old servant comes with the false news, that Orestes is dead. Electra's cry of anguish is stifled by her mother's eager, triumphant question: 'Take no heed of her, but tell me plainly in what way he died.' 'At Apollo's games in Delphi.'

That was the story he was commissioned by Orestes to tell. He means to make it credible with detail, and to wring this woman's heart. 'At the games of Delphi,' that is, not obscurely, but in the sight of Greece. He had been successful, acclaimed as the great son of a greater man, Agamemnon, captain of all Greece. That is wormwood for Clytaemnestra. On the next day, in the chariot-race, brilliant, almost victorious, within an ace of triumph, he fell from his car and was killed. The people wept for him, and burnt his body, and are sending home for burial all that is left of this beautiful strong son of hers, a heap of ashes in an urn.

Even Clytaemnestra is a mother. The old man has told his tale to some purpose. 'It is strange to be a mother. We cannot hate our children, though they hurt us.' [40] Then she draws breath again, and revels in the thought that she is safe at last. No more sleepless nights. No more fear of Electra's tongue. Electra has listened too, and believes. She has heard her mother's triumph, and the insults to the dead. She has no more strength or hope. The consolations of the Chorus are a mockery.

Chrysothemis returns with her pathetic little story of the lock of hair she has found at Agamemnon's tomb. Surely it must be Orestes? Electra stops her, but draws strength from her presence. Will not Chrysothemis help? Can they not together kill Aegisthus?

Chrysothemis draws away. She must act alone. Then Orestes comes with the urn, and when he hears her pitiful lament, is forced, in spite of danger, to reveal himself. From that moment Electra is transformed. She becomes radiant, gentle, young. Even her brother's mission is forgotten, till he reminds her. He knows that for her as well as himself her transports are dangerous. Every moment increases the risk. What does she care 'for a parcel of women indoors?' She has Orestes. She is living in a world of love and happiness.

She will obey him. She will be quiet. Her love makes her his eager, humble servant. She lives to help him. The grim old man interrupts with a reminder of the task. The moment is propitious. Clytaemnestra is alone. The men go to their work.

Electra goes with them, but returns. The Chorus have been muttering a hymn of vengeance, mixed with haunting strains of fear, recalling themes once used by Aeschylus in the tense moments before the murder of King Agamemnon. Electra stops them.

EL. Dear women, the men are at the doing. Wait in silence.

CH. What is it that you say? What are they doing?

EL. She is dressing the urn for burial, and the two stand near her.

CH. And you came out — for what?

EL. To watch, and keep Aegisthus from entering without our knowledge.

CLYT. (*within*). Alas! Home destitute of friends, full of destroyers.

EL. Someone cried out within. Did you not hear, dear women?

CH. I heard it — intolerable — woe is me — I shudder.

CLYT. (*within*). Ah me! Aegisthus, where art thou?

EL. Listen, the voice again!

CLYT. (*within*). O child, child, pity thy mother.

EL. You had no pity for him or for his father.

CH. O city, O unhappy race, now is your day of life perishing, perishing.

CLYT. (*within*). Ah me! He strikes.
EL. Strike, if you have strength, again.
CLYT. (*within*). Ah me! Again.
EL. Would it were Aegisthus too.[41]

Then this, when Orestes appears, with blood on his hands:

EL. Orestes, how fare you?
OR. In the house — well, if Apollo prophesied well.
EL. Is she dead, the wretched one?
OR. You need not fear your mother will insult you any more.
CH. Stop, for I see Aegisthus.

Hastily they make preparations to complete the work. Electra shall receive the tyrant, show him Clytaemnestra's body, covered with a pall, as if it were the body of Orestes. So he will fall into the trap. She plays her part, quietly, ruthlessly. Then Orestes reveals himself. The two men wrangle for a moment. She cannot bear it. She bids her brother make an end of words. 'When men's lives are bound to evil, what gain is there in time for a man who is to die? Kill him at once, and fling his body to the only buriers this man in decency should have — out of our sight. That, only that, can set me free from the old wrong.'

Can it? Can anything? While Orestes drives the wretched man to death, turning before he goes to preach a little lesson on the consequence of crime, the excellent effect of this example; while the Chorus sing that happiness and freedom have returned to bless the house of Atreus, Electra stands silent. What are her thoughts?

The *Electra* is, I think, the darkest of all Greek tragedies. It is also one of the noblest. The art which reckons with the ultimate tragic possibilities, helps us to live. In the world of Sophocles, men build their splendid edifice of stateliness and decency and, better still, of loyalty and love, with knowledge that at any moment the gods or circumstances or some simple human blunder may sweep the work away. Only the greatest ages, the Periclean in Greece, the Elizabethan in England, can bear to face this issue. The greatest ages exult in it.

No one is safe. Our virtues may be turned by circumstance ('by the gods,' if one thinks in terms of the old symbolism) into instruments for our destruction. Oedipus, endowed with high intelligence and with courage which demands the truth at any cost, is entangled in a maze of error, through which, with growing hope and confidence, he fights his way to light, only to find, when the last veil is down, that his life is ruined. His religious scruples, his obedience to the oracle, his patriotic energy, destroy him. At the moment when he calls himself the child of Luck, and boasts that fortune will not shame her favourite, he is in the greatest danger. He thinks himself, and other people think him, more than human. Then, in a flash of revelation, the truth comes. He sees himself as an incestuous parricide, an abomination and pollution. In his agony, he blinds himself. But the sting is not, for him or for us, in the physical, but in the moral suffering. He passes, after the first paroxysms, to a calmer, very noble vision of the desperate facts. Then, with a generosity which makes the end profoundly touching, he thinks, not of himself, but of his children. He must leave them a legacy of shame, not happiness. But he can give them this, as well:

Take this one counsel: be your prayer to live
Where fortune's modest measure is, a life
That shall be better than your father's was.[42]

It is the doctrine of the modest mind, the greatest gift. Sophocles is reinterpreting once more the religion which bids us ‘ know ourselves, and shun excess.’ Wealth and power and reputation may be denied us: if we have them, they may prove a curse. Even intelligence, though it be our light, and we must follow it, may fail. This austere religion bids us not ignore, but contemplate the accidents to which we are all subject, and ‘ being mortal, think of the last day, which all must see, and speak of no man's happiness until, without great sorrow, he has finished the course of life.’

Jocasta's beauty and frailty are contrasted with this hero's tragic strength. Oedipus will have truth without compromise, and the truth breaks him. Jocasta tries to compromise. When she hears of the prophet's accusation, she decides to tell her husband of a secret which has haunted and embittered her life. Prophets may be wrong. An oracle had told Laius — she will not say it came from Apollo, but from his ministers — that a son of hers would kill him. It was false. He was murdered by highwaymen, at a place where three roads meet. But he took her child, because he believed the oracle, and pierced his ankles, and had him thrown out to die on the mountains. So much for soothsayers!

Her quick intelligence distinguishes between the god and his ministers. Her scepticism is the result of her own tragedy. She breaks a long silence in the hope of giving her husband peace of mind. Actually she gives him the first clue which will lead to the discovery of his guilt. But even at this moment, she cannot bring herself to tell the whole truth. It was not Laius who gave the child to death. Presently we shall hear — and so will Oedipus — from the servant who was charged with the grim task:

> SERVANT. They said 'twas Laius' son. . . And yet
> Perhaps Jocasta best can answer that.
> OED. Jocasta gave it you?
> SERVANT. She gave it me.
> OED. For what?
> SERVANT. She bade me do away with it.[43]

She realizes that Oedipus must be the murderer. She tries to prevent him from sending for the one eye-witness. But his insistence cannot be resisted. She yields. 'I will send at once. Let us go in. I will do nothing but to please you.' She knows what the result must be. Even so, she will pray for 'some clean way of deliverance.' The arrival of a messenger from Corinth with news of the death of Polybus completely changes her mood. Now at any rate, she thinks, Oedipus will admit that oracles are negligible. Her prayer to Apollo is forgotten: her scepticism seems more than justified. 'Luck governs everything! There is no foreknowledge. Take life at random. Live as you best can. That's the best way.' In a few moments she hears the words which tell her that the husband for whose peace of mind she has been agonizing is, in fact, the son she sacrificed for the sake of his father's life. Still she hopes desperately to escape the revelation. If only Oedipus would listen, and leave the matter where it lies. It is impossible, and when she knows that the truth must out, she goes, as quietly and as suddenly as she came. Death is her solution. For the tragic courage of Oedipus there is no such escape.

Jocasta has a quick intelligence, but tries by an economy of truth to save Oedipus from her own horrible knowledge. The heroine of the *Trachiniae*, Deianeira, shrinks, not like Jocasta from the consequences of the truth, but from the vision, the truth itself. She has no lack of moral courage. Whenever a call is made on her heart, she is ready. She is so loving that she can not merely find excuses for her husband, Heracles, but a very beautiful sympathy for the woman, Iole, who has innocently taken her place. But she is vague-minded, intellectually incompetent. In the prologue, when she tells us how young Heracles came to rescue her from the abhorrent, monstrous river-god who wooed her, she reveals unconsciously this weakness. 'He came and fought for me, and rescued me. I cannot tell how the struggle went. I do not know. One who sat and watched and did not shrink in terror from the sight, might tell.'[44] The same timidity, the same acquiescence in half-knowledge makes her speak of her husband's life as one which 'brings him home and then takes him from home in service to another.' When the play begins, she has been for fifteen months without news of Heracles, and is miserably anxious. It is left to an old nurse to hint that vague anxiety is not the only resource. 'You have many sons. Why do you not send one of them to find out? Hyllus, the eldest, for instance?' Hyllus comes in. 'My son,' says Deianeira, 'the nurse thinks it does you no credit that you make no effort to find out about your father. . .' 'But I know — if one is to believe reports. . .' It has never occurred to her to consult him. He tells her Heracles has been for the last year a Lydian woman's slave. 'If that is true, there is nothing too strange to believe,' she thinks. 'He is now reported in Euboea, attacking the city of Eurytus.' 'But, my child, do you know, he left me an oracle about that very country!' 'What did it say? I know nothing of it.' 'That he would either end his life in this adventure, or else, if he survived, live happy. . . Go, go, and help him.' 'Mother, I will go at once. If I had known. . .'

With the news of her husband's victory and imminent return, everything, for the moment, is happiness. Her kindness to the captive girl, in whom we see at once a victim of the hero's passion, touches us. We do not stop to think that this unsuspicious nature has its dangers. A busybody tells her the facts. The girl is Iole, whom Heracles loves. Deianeira sees her own happiness at stake, and there is no lack of energy or courage now in her insistence on the truth. She can still understand and pity the child whose beauty has ruined her. Then she thinks of the Centaur's love-charm. It was given by an enemy, killed by Heracles, for attempting to assault her. She is too simple to suspect that such a present may prove dangerous. Magic, she knows, is not a proper weapon for a Greek lady. The stake is her husband's love, and she will try it.

It is, of course, a deadly poison. The robe she anoints with the supposed love-charm, and sends him as her gift of welcome, will cling, and burn his flesh, until he dies in torment. When she discovers, she withdraws and ends her life.

For us the sequel is inevitably an anti-climax. We are Deianeira's partisans. The physical agony of Heracles shocks, but does not touch us. His clamour against the jealous woman who has murdered him, intelligible as it is, sounds monstrous. Hyllus, who knows her story, tells Heracles the facts. Now, we think, Heracles will make amends. Sentimentalists as we are, we feel we can forgive him, if he is heart-broken at the thought of her pitiful, tragic love. Instead of that, he is absorbed in the contemplation of his own destiny, and the strange oracles which have foretold obscurely this incredible end. It is indeed mysterious and ironical. He has laboured for humanity and conquered many brutal creatures. By his own wife's blunder he becomes at last the victim of the long-dead Centaur, an embodiment of cruelty and lust: the victim also of his own inordinate passion. But we want to hear him say that Deianeira matters to him, as she does to us.

So strongly has this sentimental satisfaction been desired that efforts have been made to twist the meaning of the play, and so secure it. We are told, for instance, that, when Heracles bids Hyllus marry Iole, he recognizes Deianeira as his true and only mate. Nothing could be further from his thought.

Hyllus must marry Iole, he says, because no one except his son must touch the woman who has been his mate. That is what Heracles says, and we must accept it. Through Iole and Hyllus, Heracles conceives, destiny will make him the father of a race of heroes.

In creating Dido, Virgil for many readers spoilt Aeneas. Sophocles, we suspect, spoilt his play, for Deianeira. If so, it was worth while. But it is not fair to leave the matter so. If we regard the play as a drama of real life, we must admit that Heracles, the man of action and of passion, is convincing: his egoism, his strain of male brutality, though it hurts us that they make him blind to Deianeira's tragedy, are also true to life. The play would have been more pleasant if the hero had been more sympathetic: but the tragedy would have been softened. Sophocles keeps it hard.

So, forgetting Deianeira, Heracles contemplates his destiny. His end, at least, shall be great. In a spirit of exaltation, defying physical torment, he bids his son prepare the fire through which he shall attain, not immortality, but rest. Here again, it would have been easy for the poet to have made the hero see — what the audience knows — that through the ordeal of the pyre Heracles, son of Zeus, is to become a god. He has preferred to keep the future dark. Hyllus, who speaks the last word, sees no hope, no solution:

'Lift him, attendants, and forgive what I shall do, and recognize the cruelty of the gods in what is to be done. They beget children and are called their fathers, yet permit such suffering as this. No man foresees the future. The present has tears for us, and shame for the gods: but it is hardest of all to bear for him who must endure it. Come with us, maidens.

Do not linger here. You have seen a strange sad death, and you have seen a manifold mystery of anguish: and there is nothing in all this that is not Zeus.' [45]

The two remaining plays, both works of the poet's old age, are not strictly tragedies. The *Philoctetes* is a delightful romance, the *Oedipus at Colonus* a religious mystery.

Neoptolemus, a generous young soldier, is entrusted by unscrupulous politicians (the Odysseus of this play is quite unlike the Odysseus of the *Ajax*) with a task from which his instinctive honesty shrinks. At the beginning of the Trojan war, the Greeks, on the advice of Odysseus, had abandoned Philoctetes on the desolate coast of Lemnos, when his presence had become offensive to them, and his help apparently useless, since he was afflicted with a loathsome and disabling disease. Now, in the tenth year of the siege, an oracle declares that the city cannot be taken without his aid, or at any rate without the bow of Heracles, which he possesses. Odysseus knows it is useless for the Greeks to appeal for help to the man they have so shockingly maltreated. But he thinks that Neoptolemus, whom the hero has never met, may win his confidence, and either kidnap him and bring him to Troy, or at any rate deprive him of the invincible weapon. The youth, he thinks, will prove a ready tool. He takes him to Lemnos, plays on his loyalty and ambition, and provides him with a story calculated to remove suspicion from the mind of Philoctetes. The politician's narrow cunning has not reckoned with the generosity of the youth.

When Neoptolemus meets Philoctetes, he first learns from him of the wanton cruelty with which the Greeks have treated him. Odysseus had not calculated on the effect of that. Then Neoptolemus admires the fortitude with which, in spite of helplessness and pain, Philoctetes has contrived not merely to live, but to keep alive his sense of honour, his scorn for the men who had wronged him, his love for loyal comrades, like Achilles, Neoptolemus' own father, and, above all, his faith in human nature. Neoptolemus is drawn to him, and he to Neoptolemus. Even so, reluctantly, Neoptolemus carries out his orders. The hero is trapped. But, at the moment when success seems imminent, Philoctetes is attacked by a paroxysm of his old disease. He knows that, in a few moments, the agony will leave him physically helpless. He begs Neoptolemus to wait, and gives him the bow, his one most precious possession. Such confidence in his loyalty is very hard for Neoptolemus to bear. Finally, he cannot endure the strain of deception any longer. He reveals the plot. He appeals to Philoctetes to be generous. Will he not come, willingly, to help? He will be healed, welcomed, honoured: in the end he will share with Neoptolemus the fame of conquering Troy.

Philoctetes refuses. The old hatred of the Greeks is too deep to be forgotten even for the sake of this new friend. Neoptolemus has to choose between loyalty to Philoctetes and his own career. He makes his choice. He is ready, in spite of Odysseus, to go home to Greece ingloriously as the sick man's escort.

But Philoctetes, though he has resisted every argument of policy and self-interest, though he has persisted in refusal even at the cost of this young man's hope of happiness, yields at last. Heracles, his own friend, the labourer for man, now deified, comes in majestic vision, and bids him go to Troy. Friendship proved stronger than ambition for Neoptolemus. Philoctetes, schooled by his friend, must accept a life of service, and be content to help the men whom he has so deeply, and so justly hated.

Finally, in his last work, Sophocles returns to Oedipus and to Antigone, linking the mystery of their lives with memories of his own birthplace and hopes for the Athens of his ideal. The *Oedipus at Colonus* is a patriotic and religious mystery. The hero, after a life of shame and persecution, is received by Athens, welcomed in spite of his past, defended against the enemies of his own household, and vindicated in the end by the gods. Throughout the play there grows on the hero and the audience a sense that his tragic life has not been altogether without purpose. There is no shallow explanation, and not even the suggestion that the fires of passion have been purged by suffering. Oedipus curses his sons: Antigone, not Oedipus, was born for love. Oedipus is no saint, no Christian hero, but a man who feels himself abnormal, charged by his tragedy with a mysterious potency for good and evil to friends and foes. Athens receives him when the rest of the world rejects him. She defends him in his weakness. She shall find safety from his strength. The drama culminates in his majestic passage from the life of men.

III. THEIR INFLUENCE IN GREECE AND ROME

SOON after the death of Sophocles, Aristophanes produced the *Frogs,* a brilliant fantasy and a penetrating, not too scrupulous analysis of new fashions in ideas and poetry. His play is more than an indictment of Euripides, also lately dead; and it is wiser than mere panegyric of old bottles burst with the new wine of sophistry. It pleads, in the last crisis of the war, for the forgiveness of old grudges, a closing of the ranks for the salvation of the State. Recall, says Aristophanes, the spirit of Aeschylus, who fought at Marathon, and showed us the Thebans manfully defending their city, the Persians overthrown, Agamemnon leading united Greece to Troy, Orestes home from exile, Achilles wrathful in his tent, but coming to the rescue after all. Take the lesson. Recall your exiles, even Alcibiades, if he will help. Remember how the *Oresteia* ended in a festival of reconciliation.

So today, by the light of mystic torches, with hymns that echo the old triumph of Athena, let Dionysus bring the spirit of Aeschylus back to the earth.

Aeschylus, enthusiastic Athenian as he was, nowhere disparaged other Greek communities. His ideal was union among Greeks and harmony in Athens. Aristophanes had preached generosity to the allies, peace with Sparta. Now in the time of crisis, he called for an end of faction, and his choice of Aeschylus as a poet who made good citizens and soldiers proves that one aspect at any rate of the old poet's work was not forgotten.

He also uses Aeschylus as typical religious poet, and links him with the goddesses of the Mysteries who, alone among Athenian divinities, give not only help in life but hope in death. At the end of the long war, the poet suggests, Euripides, ' Intelligence, and the Critical Nostril ' offer no solution. Aeschylus, who said ' Death is the only god who does not care for gifts,' can pray, ' Demeter, who didst nurse my spirit, may I be worthy of thy Mysteries.' In his own time he was an innovator, probably suspected by the parents of the men who now suspected Euripides. He was actually accused of some impiety in connection with the Mysteries, but acquitted. All that is almost — not quite — forgotten. He now stands for the good old ways, the tried old faith. That is because so much of his teaching has been absorbed into the common stock.

Our study of Sophocles will have helped us to understand that fact. Herodotus, whose narrative reflects the mingled piety and scepticism of Ionians and Athenians in the time of Pericles, owes much to Aeschylus, and to Sophocles, who was his friend, as well. The stress he lays on the modest mean; the prominence he gives to Solon's maxim, 'Call no man happy till the end,' remind us of that friendship.[46] The recurrence throughout his work of anecdotes which look at first like digressions, but are chosen and arranged to reinforce this theme, are the work of a designer well acquainted with the Aeschylean method of accumulating effect. His vast, but orderly conception of the gathering of Persian power, the gradual absorption of the whole world, except Greece, into one overweening Empire, the fates of Cyrus, Cambyses and Darius as a prelude to the tragedy of Xerxes, owes something to the inventor of the trilogy. If Prometheus unfolds a panorama of the east for Io, and of the west for Heracles, so Herodotus, by his Lydian, Egyptian, Scythian Logoi, makes the world a background for the struggle between Greece and Persia. Finally, his conception of the great deliverance as a judgment of the gods on arrogance is Aeschylean, though he does not wrestle, as did Aeschylus, with the deeper moral problems. As a story-teller, not primarily a moralist, he often talks as if men are the puppets of destiny, claimed automatically for destruction 'if it happen that their fate is evil.' But, thanks to Aeschylus and Sophocles, the weight of destiny is lighter. The inheritor of an ancestral taint is left a better chance. The grim old cult of the dead, with its corollary of hopeless, endless vendetta, is a dying superstition. Life is still a hazard, played with loaded dice and rules half-guessed against a masked opponent. But the game is worth the candle, and the player's hand is steadier, because Aeschylus — and Homer in his time — drove the worst spectres from the lingering shadows. And the morning light is coming in through the half-open windows.

Thucydides saw the war against the Spartan League as the tragedy which in fact it was. It was because, beneath the religious and poetic symbolism, there was a true vision of life in Aeschylus, that Thucydides, when he tried to write the facts, and nothing but the facts, about the war, wrote a prose tragedy. He was not, as some critics have supposed, misled by the old symbolism, haunted by superstitious notions of 'incalculable Chance.' But he did see life more clearly as a battlefield of tragic motives and of tragic human blunders because he was a fellow-countryman of Aeschylus and Sophocles. In style he owed much to Aeschylus. The subtlety of his political psychology owed more to Sophocles and to Euripides.[47]

The influence both of Aeschylus and of Sophocles on the ideals of this generation, and also on the criticism which the failure of the ideals evoked, may easily be underestimated. Pheidias thought of Homer, when he made his statue of Olympian Zeus, but he reinterpreted the old conception in terms of a more profound and more serene religion. 'Methinks,' said Dio Chrysostom, centuries later, 'if one who is heavy-laden, who has drained the cup of sorrow, and whom sweet sleep visits no more, should stand before this image, he would forget the griefs and troubles that are incident to human life.'[48] The depth and the serenity of this religion were due in part to the audacity of Aeschylus, in part to the radiant imagination of Sophocles. Had not Aeschylus challenged the gods themselves in the name of truth and righteousness, creating for himself a nobler Zeus and a more merciful Athena, Sophocles and Pheidias could not have kept the Olympians in their place as symbols of the high and tragic destiny of man. The nephew of Pheidias, when he decorated the shrine at Olympia, chose for his theme the exploits of the son of Zeus. He showed 'Prometheus still in bonds, and Heracles borne up aloft to him.' On the throne of Zeus himself were represented 'under Sphinxes, Apollo and Artemis, shooting down the children of Niobe with arrows.'[49] This inexplicable cruelty of life, as Hyllus cried, 'is also Zeus.' It was Aeschylus who made such symbolism possible.

Nevertheless, we owe an immeasurable debt to the men who broke away from the tradition. The orgies of superstition and fanaticism which crippled Athens in the war and after, above all the martyrdom of Socrates, prove that the work of 'Mind, Intelligence, the Critical Nostril' was still needed. To Aristophanes the apostles of enlightenment seemed responsible for the corruption of the age. He was mistaken. Euripides, in his criticism of society and religious prejudice, Socrates in his persistent questioning of all glib insincerities, were heirs of Aeschylus, and, in spite of appearances, collaborators, in the history of the world, with Sophocles and with Aristophanes himself. Could Euripides have drawn his Phaedra and Polyxena, had not Aeschylus created Clytaemnestra, and Sophocles, Antigone? Could he have framed his challenge, 'If the gods do what is evil, then they are not gods,' had not Aeschylus, by poetry, not logic, stirred in him aspirations which could not be satisfied with an immoral God? Socrates called himself a missionary of Apollo. His passionate belief that men must search themselves to find the meaning of life's moral tangle was a new interpretation of the Delphic 'Know thyself.' His marvellous poise of self-control and freedom from asceticism gave new meaning to Apollo's 'Nothing to excess.' But Sophrosyne, self-knowledge, moderation, are the secrets of the Sophoclean art no less than of the Socratic life. Through Sophrosyne Sophocles could assert, unflinching, uncomplaining, the ultimate tragedy of life, which is a shadow, a misfortune, and yet — or, perhaps, therefore — could keep his vision of 'those pure and holy Laws, begotten in the Aether, Laws, wherein there dwells a god.' [50] The difference between them is of course important. No Sophoclean hero could have told the jurymen who had condemned him to the hemlock: 'You also ought to have good hope concerning death, and think this certain, that there is for a good man no evil either in life or death.' [51]

Athens fell. The great tragedians were dead, and Socrates. Aristophanes lived on, but wrote tamely. His imagination had no wings. Plato turned from poetry to prose, from drama to philosophic dialogue. The old age had had poets for teachers and had murdered Socrates. The new age should be weaned from superstition and guided by philosophers. That too was an experiment which failed. Plato, like Athens, had his Sicilian expedition. But the failure was heroic. The city of Pericles fell by the defect of human nature. The Republic of Plato, happily, was never realized. But his dialectic is the instrument of modern thought, and the inspiration of his poetic vision lives.

He was reared in sight of the Acropolis, and nurtured by the wisdom of Homer, Aeschylus and Sophocles. He heard their rhythms long before he talked with Socrates or studied mathematics. Whether or not he knew it, he was remembering his own childhood when he bade his ideal city look for artists able to track out the nature of the beautiful, 'that, dwelling in a healthy place, the young may benefit, whenever from these beautiful works there comes to eyes or ears a breeze that brings them health from a good country, and insensibly from childhood onward leads them to be in tune with beauty, to love it, and grow like it.'[52] He has no desire to banish art from this city of the wise and good. Only, unfortunately, no good artist could accept the terms he offers. 'We must admonish — nay, we must compel — the poets to put into their works the image of the good character, or else not make poetry here.' Socrates might have saved himself by a promise to keep silent. 'If I tell you that to hold my peace is to disobey the god, you will not believe me. You will think it is my irony.'[53]

Reluctantly Plato banished the poets whose inspiration he could not control, though he loved and quoted them. 'We must not allow our young people to hear, as Aeschylus puts it, that God breeds a cause for men when he desireth to destroy a household. If anyone makes a poem about Niobe's suffering or the woes of Pelops' line or Troy, we must not allow these things to be described as the work of any god . . or else we must say that the god did what was just and good, and they were benefited by being destroyed.' [54] It is all grotesquely unfair, and Plato has his share of responsibility for the divorce of Christianity and art in the dark ages.

To Sophocles he is gentle. In the first scene of the *Republic,* before he launches into the ideal, he draws a picture of the present Athens at her best. It is a portrait of old Cephalus, the embodiment of Sophrosyne. The old man's talk is of Sophocles and his sweet reasonableness.[55] Happily Cephalus retires to his sacrifice before the blatant Thrasymachus has begun to scoff at justice, and before Socrates blasphemes against the poets.

While Plato's genius 'shook from its wings the materialistic bonds that clogged both thought and speech, and rose triumphant to the sphere of the colourless and formless and intangible,' [56] the Athenians went on acting tragedy, and theatres sprang up throughout the Greek world. Euripides became the favourite poet of Greece, next to Homer. Aeschylus fell into the background, though his plays were occasionally still acted. Already in the *Frogs* there are premonitions of the time when Attic ears will find his diction uncouth and unintelligible. The lyrical art, though not dead, was dying. The large and subtle symmetry of his odes could not compete with the bravura of Euripides, the programme-music of Timotheus. In the *Clouds*, the young man, fresh from the Thinking-Shop, finds him 'Full of sound, amorphous, a mouther . . ,' and the phrase became a commonplace of criticism. Quintilian translates it: 'Aeschylus invented Tragedy. He is sublime, grandiloquent, often to a fault, and for the most part rugged, ill-composed. And for that reason the Athenians allowed the later poets to produce corrected versions of his plays in competition.'[57] We should be glad to know what the corrected versions were like. We are grateful to Lycurgus for establishing an official text about 330 B.C.

Sophocles held the stage, though he too naturally paled before the philosophic, sentimental poet. Demosthenes learnt elocution from an actor who recommended declamation from Sophocles. His opponent Aeschines was an actor and played Creon in the *Antigone*. Antipater's agent, who brought him to bay at last, was an actor too; and the orator, when he drank the poison, cried to the would-be assassin: 'Take up your old rôle of Creon, and have my body thrown where you will without burial.' This man, Archias, taught the famous Polus, who made Electra's recognition-scene so moving by declaiming with the urn of his dead son in his hand. No one seems to have felt it was a sentimental outrage. Aristippus, shipwrecked on the Sicilian coast, quoted the first lines of the *Oedipus at Colonus*. Polemo, the Academic, thought Sophocles 'the tragic Homer' and his style like a good wine, neither too sweet nor too dry. The Stoic Cleanthes, the author of the *Hymn to Zeus* — and in that an inheritor of Aeschylus—stamped on the ground when a sick Stoic friend grew impatient of suffering, and cried: 'Do you hear, Amphiaraus, below?' It was a quotation from Aeschylus or Sophocles, and was meant to remind the inconsistent Stoic of the master Zeno. The swashbuckler Demetrius Poliorcetes quoted Aeschylus when he was defeated; and a mutinous subordinate turned on him, when he had led the army into a tight place, with a parody of *Oedipus at Colonus:* 'Child of the blind old man, Antigonus, where have you brought us?' But the favourite poet of the age was Euripides, and Menander's polished comedy was the direct descendant of his work. Aristotle was exceptional in his preference for Sophocles, and that fact alone, at such a time, was a clear proof of his acuteness as a critic.[58]

Meanwhile, Alexander the Great was conquering the East, and founding Alexandria (331 B.C.). Here the Ptolemies tried in vain to foster a revival of the drama. Philadelphus had his 'tragic Pleiad.' Alexander the Aetolian kept the tragic books, as Zenodotus, the Homeric, Lycophron, the comic. To grammarians like Aristophanes and Aristarchus we owe something for our knowledge of Athenian production. These men kept the text for us, and handed on traditions of interpretation. It is hardly fair to quote the learned imbecilities of Lycophron's *Cassandra* as evidence of Alexandrian taste in tragedy. Still, Aeschylus and Sophocles, divorced from the theatre, and appealing to a little company of pedants, were only half alive.

Thanks to the survival of a living Greek Theatre in South Italy, Greek Tragedy found its way to Rome, and there inspired a living Roman drama. The vitality of the new birth is proved by a long succession of illustrious names — Livius Andronicus, a Greek freedman, whose first Roman play was acted in 240 B.C.; Naevius, Ennius, Pacuvius, his nephew, who lived on into the time of the Gracchi; and Accius, the last, and perhaps the greatest, who read his *Atreus* to the old Pacuvius, and lived long enough to talk with Cicero.

Of their work we have only fragments, but enough to show that it was strong and passionate. They plundered and adapted Aeschylus and Sophocles, but most of all Euripides, freely, not as academic imitators. It is a Roman poet, not a mere imitator, who announces as his subject, the old tale of Pelops' line:

> *inimicitias Pelopidum*
> *Extinctas pausa, oblitteratas memoria* [59]

and describes Philoctetes, deserted:

> [*iaceo*] *in tecto umido,*
> *quod eiulatu questu gemitu fremitibus*
> *resonando mutum flebilis voces refert.*[60]

It is an Italian, though the inspiration comes from Aeschylus, who writes:

caelum nitescere, arbores frondescere,
vites laetificae pampinis pubescere. . .[61]

Until the fall of the Republic the theatre was even a living force in politics. When Aesopus played the exiled Telamon, the audience cried out for the return of Cicero. At the funeral games of Caesar, when the *Ajax* of Pacuvius was performed, they demanded a thousand repetitions of the line:

Men' me servasse ut essent qui me perderent.

Cicero, following Accius, made a version of the complaint of Heracles from the *Trachiniae,* and a fine translation of some passages in the lost sequel to the *Prometheus:*

Titanum soboles, socia nostri sanguinis,
Generata coelo. . .[62]

His brother Quintus, bored with military duty in Gaul and Britain, begged for books from Rome, and amused himself by writing tragedies — no less than four in sixteen days, if Cicero is serious. Pompey quoted Sophocles to Cornelia, as he stepped down from his ship into the boat in which he was to be murdered by the treacherous Egyptians. Caesar wrote an *Oedipus,* Maecenas a *Prometheus,* and Augustus began an *Ajax.* Someone asked him how it was progressing, and he answered: 'Ajax has fallen on a sponge.'

The stories, the sentiments, sometimes the phrases of Greek Tragedy can still be recognized as part of the materials exploited, in their different ways, by nearly all the Latin poets. Lucretius draws hints from Aeschylus as well as from Euripides for his unforgettable Iphigeneia.[63] Horace's Hypermestra, *splendide mendax,* and his Teucer — *nil desperandum Teucro duce* — spring ultimately from Aeschylus and Sophocles. His just and pertinacious hero who cares nothing for the tyrant or the mob is Roman; but the original is Prometheus:

> *Si fractus illabatur orbis,*
> *Impavidum ferient ruinae.*[64]

Ajax in Sophocles gave Accius the phrase 'Virtuti sis par, dispar fortunis patris'; and Virgil remembers both when his Aeneas bids Ascanius,

Disce, puer, virtutem ex me verumque laborem,
Fortunam ex aliis.[65]

Ovid, of course, is full of tragic reminiscences. He compared himself in exile to Philoctetes. His verses kept the Greek stories alive in Europe when Greek itself was practically forgotten.[66] But the spirit is more important than the matter. Plutarch drank deep of Homer and Greek Tragedy. The tragic forces still dominate his heroic world and his discussion on the human passions and the dispensations of the gods in the *Moralia*. Plato and Stoicism and a hundred other influences contribute, but much of the old virile tragic view remains. This garrulous, old-fashioned moralist, far more than Ovid and even Seneca, has the honour to be a link between Greek tragedy and Shakespeare.

The rejection of Greek poetry by the Church was unfortunate, but not inevitable. Clement of Alexandria, Platonizing his Christianity, quotes passage after passage of the tragedians, sometimes to show that they are wrong, more often to illustrate his favourite doctrine that the wisdom of the Greeks was a divinely ordered preparation of men's minds for Christ.

He probably derived much of his knowledge from anthologies, and too often he falls a victim to the charms of pious forgeries, made, it is thought, by learned Jews in Alexandria. Still his gentle reconciliation of the old and new is better worth remembering than Tertullian's vindictive rhetoric, which swamps in one vituperative flood 'the madness of the circus, the immodesty of the theatre, the atrocities of the arena, and the useless exercises of the wrestling-ground.' For Tertullian the theatres are temples of Venus and Bacchus; the devil gave men artistic gifts to entice them away from God; the devil made the tragic actor wear the buskin, because Christ said 'You cannot add a cubit to your stature,' and the devil wanted to refute it. Yet he pays an unconscious tribute to the imaginative appeal of the old poetry, when he says that God is the true Prometheus, who gave order to the world. Even he must admit that sometimes the theatre offers things agreeable and innocent. Of course — 'the devil puts things of God into his honeyed draught. . . Everything there that is brave or noble or high-sounding or melodious or exquisite in taste, is to be counted as a drop of honey in a poisoned cake.' [67]

Meanwhile Tragedy had withdrawn from the public stage to Seneca's closet. On the stage the dancers enacted the old stories in wordless pantomime. The cycle which began in the old dancing-places of Crete seemed complete and finished, forever.

PART II

MODERN INFLUENCES

PART II
MODERN INFLUENCES

IV. THE REBIRTH IN ITALY

IN THE West, on the whole, the spirit of Tertullian had prevailed, though Tertullian himself had been declared a heretic. Not only ecclesiastical discouragement of pagan art, but the gradual crumbling of society, impoverishment, loss of public spirit, and barbarian invasions, led to the dark ages. In Byzantium a few Greek plays continued to be read, and scholars kept the tradition alive. Manuscripts were written, and to the very eve of the Italian renaissance, men like Triclinius were commenting, not ignorantly, on the texts. Even in the West the Latin classics were not quite forgotten, and through them, however obscurely, some trace of the tragic myths and sentiments persisted.

For centuries men spoke of Virgil reverently as a magician and a prophet of the Messiah. Dante read him as a poet, and modern literature was born. He knew no Greek, and, though he names Euripides, he does not mention Aeschylus or Sophocles. Even so, he has caught some echoes of their poetry through Virgil, Ovid, Lucan, Statius and Cicero.

> O *Niobe, con che occhi dolenti*
> *vedeva io te. . .*[68]

He read of her in Ovid; but it was Aeschylus who made her story famous. In the planetary heaven of the inconstant moon is Jephthah, unstable, like the Aeschylean Agamemnon —

> *lo gran duca dei Greci,*
> *Onde pianse Ifigenia il suo bel volto. . .*[68]

Therefore, ye Christians, be not 'like a feather, moved by every wind.' The links are Aeschylus, Euripides, Lucretius, Cicero, Ovid, Dante. Dante's genius adorns his reminiscence with an image used, in the same sense, by the only poet in the series who is Dante's peer.

When Petrarch died, he was making notes in his Latin Homer, a crude version made for him by Leonzio Pilato. In the letter which expresses his delight at the dim vision of the *Iliad* thus vouchsafed him, he refers to the unknown Sophocles. He cannot believe, he says, that the poet died, as some allege, for joy at victory in a dramatic contest. 'I am unwilling to be-

SOPHOCLES
ROME, LATERAN MUSEUM

lieve that grief and joy, those most disturbing passions, could have held such sway over divine intelligences.' He begged Leonzio, when he left Italy on his last voyage to the East, to purchase him a copy of Euripides and Sophocles. When he heard that the unhappy man had been struck dead by lightning just before his ship came safe to Venice, he hurried to the waterside in the hope that his request might have been remembered and the treasure be found on board. Seneca he knew; and Terence he had given as a present to Leonzio. But neither he nor Boccaccio knew the Greek dramatists.[69]

In 1396, Chrysoloras began to teach the elements of Greek at Florence. Vergerius threw up his professorship at Padua to attend this course, and, afterwards, by his treatise on the training of the character, inspired the greatest teacher of the age, Vittorino, the well-loved founder of that happy school, La Giocosa, where, as Flecker says, 'he taught his Mantuans the rhythm of body and mind.'[70] Both Vittorino at Mantua and Guarino at Ferrara made the Greek dramatists a part of their regular course. We are told that Aeschylus was Vittorino's favourite. We may be sure he valued his manly, patriotic spirit and his grave, religious feeling; his art, in view both of the state of the text and of his own comparatively limited Greek, he can hardly have appreciated.[71] Manuscripts were still rare and precious. Did Vittorino get his Aeschylus from the Sicilian Aurispa, who sold him in 1425, we know, a Plutarch, and 'as fine a copy of Plato' as the merchant ever saw? Anyhow it was Aurispa who, in 1422–3, was gathering manuscripts in Constantinople, and sent home the famous codex known as the Laurentian manuscript of Sophocles, the Medicean of Aeschylus. He bought it for that elegant copyist, Niccolo dei Niccoli of Florence, a collector worthy to possess it, for he was himself, like Sophocles, 'a being of beautiful presence, with a quiet smile playing about his lips.'[72] His friend the good monk Traversari, when he saw it, declared he had never seen a handsomer book of poetry. After Niccoli's death in 1437 the manuscript found a home in San Marco, where Savonarola was to reign. Happily it escaped the bonfire of vanities. At the beginning of the next century it was taken to Rome by Leo X, but Clement VII restored it to Florence, where it still adorns his Laurentian Library.[73]

Meanwhile, an event occurred more important than the recovery of any manuscript. In 1502 the seven plays of Sophocles were printed by Aldus in Venice. This first edition was dedicated to Janus Lascaris, appropriately enough, since Lascaris had lectured on Sophocles in Florence, and was now a missionary of humanism in France. The editor describes how an affectionate and respectful talk of a band of scholars round a winter fire in Venice led to the dedication.[74] In 1503 appeared the Aldine Euripides, in 1508 the first edition of the *Poetics,* and in 1518, from the same house, though the great printer was dead, the first edition of Aeschylus. It would be pleasant to dwell on the activities of this Venetian circle, but we pass on, remembering the instruction which the busy Aldus placed above his door as a warning to visitors: 'Do thy business in briefest wise, and then at once depart.' But we cannot go without mentioning one more Italian scholar, the greatest of them all, Victorius, who gave the world the first edition which contained the full text of the *Agamemnon.*[75]

Venice gave us the first texts. Meanwhile, her ally Vicenza, in the miserable war of the

League of Cambrai, suffered plague and siege and pillage. The spirit with which her citizens reacted was heroic. Faction forgotten, noble families vied with each other in the work of building a yet nobler city. The title of Trissino's poem, *Italia Liberata dai Goti,* is like a trumpet-call. We smile when we are told the pedant's purpose was to show his knowledge of the military art as practised in antiquity. His purpose was to show that Italy, in spite of disasters, could still hope by courage and high thoughts to rival ancient Greece and Rome. In that spirit he composed the first Tragedy in the vernacular. *Sofonisba* broke the dull succession of Latin, Senecan, imitations. It was the first Italian tragedy, and it drew inspiration from Euripides and Sophocles.

That was in 1515. Later in life, Trissino, as an architect and a student of Vitruvius, gave himself to the remodelling of his villa at Cricoli, on classical designs. Among the workers was the young Palladio, whose genius Trissino recognized. Of Palladio's career this is not the place to speak. But his last and not least imposing work was the Olympic Theatre which is still the glory of Vicenza. In 1561 a brilliant company had witnessed on a temporary wooden structure, made from Palladio's design, a revival of *Sofonisba.* The desire arose to build a permanent theatre. The community gave a site; subscriptions poured in from Academies all over Italy. The architect died before the work was finished. But in 1585, the Theatre, dedicated by the Olympic Academy 'Virtuti ac Genio,' was inaugurated by a performance in Italian of the *Oedipus Tyrannus.* Oedipus was played by Luigi Groto, who was blind. The part has been played there several times since, notably by Salvini. It is said that, when Napoleon entered this theatre, he turned to the Queen of Bavaria and cried: 'Madam, we are in Greece.'[76]

In spite of brilliant episodes, Greek drama claims comparatively little influence on the literature of the Italian renaissance. Plato, not Sophocles, was the saint of the Florentine Academy. In the main the inspiration of Italian literature at this time was naturally Latin and Italian. But the torch which Italy relighted was to kindle a generous flame in France and England.

V. THE REBIRTH IN FRANCE

IN FRANCE, says Gargantua, 'since printing was discovered, by divine inspiration, as by diabolical suggestion on the other side was the invention of ordnance,' the rubbish of the people have become more learned than the doctors and preachers of his own young days. As for Greek, a man may be ashamed to account himself a scholar without it.[77] But Rabelais, with all his learning, does not mention Aeschylus or Sophocles. Thanks to Dorat and Turnebus, the poets of the younger generation knew them well. Both these scholars are named in Montaigne's well-known list of 'artificers in poesie.'[78] These artificers not only vied in Latin with the Italians, but were begetters, through Greek scholarship and human sympathy, of French poetry in Ronsard and du Bellay, Baïf and Jodelle. Turnebus is well known as the editor of Aeschylus, the scholar of whom both Ronsard and Montaigne declared he had no pedantry about him, except the way he wore his gown. But Dorat's influence was greater. He published hardly anything except his Latin poems — and many of these are in praise of other people's work. But the fruits of his modest labour were eagerly recorded in the margins of their books by men like Joseph Scaliger and Canter and Lambinus, thence, in the seventeenth century pirated by Stanley, but restored to their true owner after many days by Blomfield, and crowned by Hermann and by Walter Headlam with judicious praise. But he was more than a great emender of dark texts. Ronsard, du Bellay and the rest admired and loved him. A generous spirit inhabited the puny body, and the light of genius touched the rugged toil-worn face with beauty.

Ronsard was a youth of sixteen, living in a world of poetry ruled by Horace, Ovid, Virgil and the Italians, when good fortune recommended him to the notice of an eminent humanist who was also a man of affairs. Lazare de Baïf had been the King's ambassador in Venice, and was now on his way to Germany on diplomatic business. In his company Ronsard saw such men as Sturmer, Bucer, Calvin. But better than this introduction to the great world was the invitation which de Baïf gave him two years later to share the studies of his son, Jean-Antoine, under Dorat. At that time, 1544, Dorat was forty-five years old, Ronsard eighteen. Presently, when Dorat was appointed Professor at the Collège de Coqueret, the young men renounced the pleasures and ambitions of the court to follow him. He became the friend, the boon-companion, the oracle of the Brigade, the 'Musagetes' of the Pleiad.[79]

There are pleasant and unpleasant ways of learning even grammar. Dorat's pupils learnt the elements from the *Hecuba*. Every day, after their lesson, they would report to Jean-Antoine's father, and would turn the passage they had studied, for the ambassador's 'pleasure and recreation,' word for word from Greek to Latin. Lazare was moved by 'the sublimity of style and gravity of sentiment' to turn the play into the King's French, and he published it anonymously with a dedication to the King. Seven years before, he had done the *Electra* of Sophocles into French verse, a notable achievement. This turning into French, not Latin, is what matters.[80]

Dorat recognized his pupil's genius. 'Desiring that his spirit should be nursed with appropriate aliment,' he read him 'à plein vol' the whole of the *Prometheus,* making a version for him. That was better even than to have edited the play.[81] The pupil cried: 'Et quoî, mon maître, m'avez-vous si longtemps caché ces richesses?', and went off to translate the *Plutus* into French — the first comedy, we are told, performed in the French tongue. Aeschylus, Aristophanes and Pindar are 'appropriate aliment' for the lyrical imagination. Dorat knew. He taught his pupils to discriminate among the Latins, and to read Greek abundantly — too indiscriminately, say some modern critics. There was rubbish as well as gold in learning's treasure-house. Lycophron's Cassandra raves erudition, and as Dorat said (apparently without a touch of irony), indubitably she is mad. It does not matter. Ronsard, like Aeschylus, Callimachus, and Milton, revelled in a wealth of allusion, an accumulation of sonorous epithets and fine periphrases. But his style is clear, his thought direct, his imagination true. 'Pillage the sacred treasure of this Delphic temple without scruple,' cries du Bellay to the modern Gauls. 'Away with all our fears of this dead Apollo, his false oracles, his blunted arrows.'[82] Ronsard pillaged well, and gave a point to many of the blunted shafts he stole.

His music is irresistible even to an English ear.

Of course the Pleiad had to have its dramatist. Jean-Antoine, as his father's son, seemed an obvious candidate, and he thought of writing a *Cleopatra;* du Bellay looked on him as a future Euripides, and Ronsard, thinking of a greater than Euripides, foretold for him the glory of a tragic song, 'clamorous with grief, and loud with long-drawn thunders.' When Jodelle achieved the success of which de Baïf dreamt, de Baïf hailed his friend's achievement, and decided to abandon tragic ambitions. He was in love, and for a lover 'the piteous end of the brave sons of Priam, the blood-stained line of Pelops, and the blinding of him who was the brother of his sons' — Thebes, Pelops' line and Troy, in fact — are no fit themes.

But the impulse returned. He wrote not only comedies, but translations, now lost, of the *Trachiniae* and the *Medea,* and an excellent version of the *Antigone,* which survives. It was printed in 1573, but probably composed much earlier. The dialogue follows Sophocles faithfully. The chorus is treated freely. The general result is not a slavish imitation, but a living play for a French audience. This is how de Baïf makes the selfish, very human Watchman talk about his hesitation to face Creon:

Car mon coeur me disait: Chétif que veux-tu faire?
Tu vas de ce forfait pourchasser le salaire.
Chétif, demourras-tu?

Who can help thinking of Lancelot Gobbo? [83]

Jodelle made something better than the most spirited translation. His *Cleopatra,*[84] played before the King in 1552, amid the plaudits of the court, the poets and the scholars, was original, and it had passion. Dorat and his other friends were right to celebrate this triumph as the rebirth of a sacred art in France. We like them none the less for the tales that gossip whispered of their rustic festival, their praise of Dionysus, their 'sacrifice' of a symbolic, flower-crowned goat. Actually, they did not kill the animal, but presented it, with gilded horns and beard, to Jodelle as the tragic prize, then drove it away, like an ancient scapegoat. It was indeed a great occasion. The stark sincerity of Jodelle's tragedy is worth more than all the Senecan repertoire of a Grévin and a Garnier.

The ghost of Antony prologizes — that sounds Senecan. But his words come from his heart, and the effect of his appearance, a dream-vision calling Cleopatra, is not Senecan at all. Euripides has a hand — and so has Sophocles — in these first lines of the first original French tragedy:

Dans le val tenebreux où les nuicts eternelles
Font eternelle peine aux ombres criminelles,
Cedant a mon destin, je suis volé n'aguère,
Jà jà fait compagnon de la troupe legère,
Moy, dis-je, Marc-Antoine, horreur de la grand
Romme,
Mais en ma triste fin cent fois misérable homme.

That is Sophoclean. He is another Ajax. But his ruin came from a passion which will be the theme of a greater poet than Jodelle —

un ardent amour, bourreau de mes moüelles,
Me devorant sans fin. . .

He remembers the beginning of his love, how it tortured him, like a Prometheus; how it earned him the hate of Rome, and how he sacrificed for Cleopatra not only Rome, but Caesar's friendship, and even his own wife and children:

E*t mes mollets enfans je vins chasser arrière,*
N*ourissant en mon sein ma serpente meurdrière.*

Memories crowd on him, until they reach a climax, not of indignation, but of love and pity:

César mesme n'eust peu regarder Cléopâtre
Couper sur moy son poil, se deschirer et battre,
E*t moy la consoler avecques ma parole,*
M*a pauvre âme soufflant qui tout soudain s'en-*
vole. . .

He has come to bid her bury him and follow, rather than be led in Roman triumph:

L'*ayant par le desir de la mort confortée,*
L'*appelant avec moy. . .*

He vanishes. Cleopatra wakes and tells her women of her own memories, his sacrifices, his heroism, and his death. She faints at the thought of it. Her maids revive her.

ERAS. Soulagez votre peine,
Efforcez vos esprits.
CLEOP. Las! Las!
CHARMIUM. Tenez la resne. . .

Then she speaks of her dream, and her determination to die.

A Roman scene follows. Octavian's grief for Antony makes us feel the greatness of both men. His councillors remind him of his wrongs, and urge him to be firm. The Queen may try to take her life.

Cleopatra and Octavian meet. For her children's sake, she tries to conciliate him, and pretends that she means to live. Love, she admits, has been the cause of all her policy . .

Veu qu'il fallait rompre paix et combattre
Ou separer Antoine et Cléopâtre —
Separer — las! ce mot me fait faillir. . .

OCT. Si je n'etais ore
Assex bening, vous pourriez feindre encore
Plus de douleurs, pour plus bening me rendre.
Mais quoy! ne veux-je à mon merci vous prendre?

CLEOP. Feindre, hélas! Ô!

The sudden violence of her assault on a disloyal slave who accuses her of hiding some of the royal treasures, completes the character.

She tricks Octavian, does the last rites for Antony, and goes to die.

The last Act suffers from the traditional *ne coram populo,* and from a sententiousness which does recall the method of Seneca. But the scene which the Roman found, when the doors burst open and he entered the Queen's chamber, is memorable for its Sophoclean reserve, and for its kinship — not in form but spirit — with the work of a greater poet even than Sophocles:

> E*t qu'en entrant en ceste chambre close,*
> J'*ay veu — ô rare et miserable chose!—*
> M*a Cléopâtre en son royal habit,*
> E*t sa couronne, au long d'un riche lict*
> P*eint et doré, blesme et morte couchée,*
> S*ans qu'elle fust d'aucun glaive touchée,*
> A*vecq Eras, sa femme, à ses pieds morte,*
> E*t Charmium vive, qu'en telle sorte*
> J'*ay lors blasmée: A a! Charmium, est-ce*
> N*oblement faict? Ouy, ouy, c'est de noblesse*
> D*e tant de rois Egyptiens venuë*
> U*n temoignage.*[85]

The King gave Jodelle many compliments, and five hundred crowns from his purse. And no wonder, says Pasquier, who was present, sitting with Turnebus: 'c'était chose nouvelle, et très belle, et très rare.'

VI. ELIZABETHANS

ON A December afternoon in 1563 Sir William Cecil, afterwards Lord Burghley, gave a dinner-party at Windsor Castle. He had once taught Greek at Cambridge, and the names of his guests remind us that in those days the Queen's business was done by scholars. There was Mr. Haddon, for instance, once the Master first of a Cambridge, then of an Oxford College, now a trusted statesman. When the Queen was asked if she thought him as learned as the famous Scot, Buchanan, she answered with her customary adroitness that she put Buchanan before all others and Haddon below none. She used his knowledge of the law, and liked him well for his plain speaking. When she cried 'Your new boots stink,' he said, 'I think, Madam, it is not my new boots stink, but the old petitions which have been so long in my bag unopened.' There was Astley, with his memories of talk about the Classics in his youth at Chelsea and Hatfield and of his exile with the English Protestants at Frankfurt. There was Sir Walter Mildmay, from whose College of Emmanuel (founded 1584) were to come those scholars and divines who were to make New England, in Cotton Mather's phrase, 'Emmanuel's Land indeed.' And there was Mr. Roger Ascham.[86]

After dinner Ascham went to read Demosthenes and Aeschines with the Queen, who would read at Windsor, besides Latin, Italian, French and English, 'more Greek every day than some Prebendaries of this Church doth read Latin in a whole week.' When he came back, Sir Richard Sackville asked him for advice about his little grandson's education. Could he not be taught with Ascham's son? If Ascham found the tutor, Sackville would defray the expense. Such an offer from the Chancellor of the Exchequer, who was called by unkind critics Richard Sack-Fill, was acceptable. To the conversation of that memorable evening we owe Ascham's *Scholemaster*. It begins with a tribute to Sir John Cheke, Ascham's teacher, and King Edward's, and with a compliment to Sackville. Cheke at Cambridge had lectured steadily through Sophocles, and his pupil makes a courtly use of the memory by applying to his benefactor 'that sweet verse of Sophocles, spoken by Oedipus to the worthie Theseus: "What I have I owe to you, and to no other mortal man."'[87]

Education should aim, he says, at truth of religion, honesty in living and right order in learning. Literature is necessary food for a young mind. 'Marke all Mathematicalle heades, which be onely and wholly bent to those sciences, how solitarie they be themselves, how unfit to live with others, and how unapte to serve in the world.' And of authors, all, as compared with Greek — Cicero only excepted, and one or two more in Latin — are 'patched cloutes and ragges in comparison of faire woven broade-clothes.' 'Learning is difficult, but Labor always obtaineth his purposes, as Aristotle his Rhetoric and Oedipus in Sophocles[88] do teach.' Above all, in Tragedy the Greeks excel:

In Tragedies — the goodliest argument of all, and for the use, either of a learned preacher, or a civill gentleman, more profitable than Homer, Pindar, Virgill and Horace: yea, comparable in myne opinion with the doctrine of Aristotle, Plato and Xenophon — the Grecians, Sophocles and Euripides, far outmatch our Seneca in Latin, namely in oikonomia et decoro, though Seneca's elocution and his verse be verie commendable for his tyme.

There is a touch of pedantry, but the preference for Sophocles in an age which was eagerly exploiting Seneca is original. Only two years before this Windsor party, Sir Richard's son, the little grandson's father, Thomas Sackville, had produced with Norton at Whitehall before the Queen, the first original English tragedy, the Senecan *Gorboduc*. And in 1564 Marlowe and Shakespeare were to be born.

Ascham's preference for Greek was genuine, and based on knowledge. At Cambridge he had 'many pleasant talks' with Cheke on 'the true difference of authors,' comparing Seneca, Euripides and Sophocles. He had made a book of specimens to show the difference. So Greek was teaching the best minds of England to ask for something better than Seneca's fustian. We smile at the scholar's contempt for 'Gothic rhyming,' and his scorn for the Cambridge man, 'well liked of many, but best liked of himself,' who looked to win his spurs with a play of which the Protasis began with eight-footed trochaics. Ascham saw, at any rate, that

Greek hexameters will not suit our tongue—they ‘ trot and hobble,’ he says, in English; and he prophesied the triumph of blank verse. Above all, his own prose shows the influence of Greek harmonies and Greek ideas:

No perfection is durable. Encrease hath a time, and decay likewise, but all perfit ripenesse remaineth but a moment: as is plainly seen in fruits, plummes and cherries: but more sensibly in flowers, as Roses and such like, and yet as trewlie in all greater matters. For what naturallie can go no hier, must naturallie yield and stoupe again.

The plums and cherries grew in English orchards: the roses bloomed and faded at Paestum and in Greece: and the thought, applied to greater matters, is the central thought of Sophocles. When Greek poetry and English life had taught a schoolmaster to write like this, the time of ‘ perfit ripenesse ’ was not far away for English poetry. At the Universities the time of blossoming in Greek was short. The monasteries had supported students, and their suppression had already caused a shrinking in the number of the pupils. The success of the new learning had drawn men like Cheke and Smith and Cecil into the great world: the smaller men remained as teachers. Above all, the weariness and dangers of disputes about theology, the quarrels first between Pope's men and King's men, then between surplice-men and puritans, embittered minds, and turned them from sweet learning to bad logic, sour divinity. But Greek was taught, and many people got a smattering.

Ascham refers in *Toxophilus* to the bowmen of the *Persae,* and he had, no doubt, read Aeschylus. But Sophocles and Euripides, not Aeschylus, were for him the obvious models of Greek Tragedy. That is not surprising. The good fortune which brought Ronsard and his circle into direct touch with the best Greek scholars in Europe was exceptional. Dorat's pupils were better able to understand Aeschylus than any poet-scholars before Milton.

In England texts must have been rare, and complete texts rarer still. When Turnebus published his edition in 1552 — the year of Jodelle's triumph — he admitted the extreme difficulty of his task. He had often, he says, been overcome by a speechlessness, and found himself unable to solve the textual problems — he had left what he knew to be 'gangrenous words,' thinking it better to leave the difficulties than to jump at easy solutions. Robortelli wrote in a similar strain in Venice, in the same year. Even after Turnebus, Victorius and Canter had done their excellent work, Salmasius, Milton's contemporary and opponent, coined the well-known phrase (printed by Stanley as a motto to his own edition in 1663) about the obscurity of the *Agamemnon,* surpassing 'all the sacred writings, with their Hebraisms, Syriasms, and all that Hellenistic bag and baggage.' The *Prometheus,* the *Persae,* and, to some extent, the *Eumenides,* were fairly plain sailing, and their influence was considerable. But the difficulties which beset even scholars when they tried to see the *Oresteia* as a whole seemed overwhelming.

We must be cautious when, for instance, Churton Collins [89] asks us to believe that Shakespeare may have drawn ideas from the Aeschylean Clytaemnestra for his Lady Macbeth. Why should he not have read the Latin version by Sanravius, published at Basel in 1555? The answer is that, if he had seen this version, he could not have gathered from it even the plot of the *Agamemnon.* That play was not even published in a complete Greek text before Victorius' Paris edition of 1557. Sanravius' version, based inevitably on the earlier, defective texts, telescoped part of the *Agamemnon* and part of the *Libation-Bearers* into one dramatically unintelligible play. No sooner has the beacon-speech (which is assigned, by the way, to a Messenger, not to the Queen) reached its climax 'So the fire . . swooped on this palace-roof,' than we find the Chorus saying 'I, because I pity, will not be angry,' and Cassandra shouting 'O to to tae, popae, da.' And again, Cassandra's visions are surprisingly cut short. 'I was reared,' she wails, 'by the waters of Scamander,' when Orestes, of all people, stops her with the question: 'What do I see? Who are these women robed in black. . . ?' They are the Trojan captives and Electra, bringing Clytaemnestra's offerings to the tomb. No wonder Scaliger remarked that there are violations of probability in Aeschylus. 'Agamemnon,' he complains, 'is murdered and buried all of a sudden, so that the actor has hardly time to breathe.' The correct edition of Victorius came too late to enlighten him.

Of course, if Shakespeare knew as much Greek as, for instance, Peele and Marlowe, and if he had the luck to read Aeschylus in Victorius' edition, or — which would perhaps be more probable — in Canter's of 1580, this particular difficulty would not arise. But, if we are talking of the influence of Latin versions, we must be careful.

I have before me a little fat volume, printed by Stephanus in 1567, which contains the most popular Greek plays of the Renaissance, done into Latin. First come *Hecuba* and *Iphigeneia at Aulis*, in Erasmus' version, then Buchanan's *Medea* and *Alcestis;* then, for Sophocles, *Ajax, Electra* and *Antigone*, in the version of the young Dutch lawyer, Rotaller, published first at Louvain, 1548; and last, the ever popular *Prometheus*, the one play of Aeschylus, in a good version by Garbitius. For the plays by Euripides and Sophocles, this excellent little book provides, not only the Greek text and Latin verse translation, but a literal Latin prose crib. Nothing is more likely than that a well-read Englishman of Shakespeare's time should have read any or all of these plays.

The illustrious band of poets who enriched the English tongue with melody in Shakespeare's youth were known as University Wits: Lyly and Sidney, Peele and Lodge of Oxford, Spenser, Greene and Nash and Marlowe of

Cambridge. The Greek and Latin which was read, and the academic plays which were acted, at the universities, were among the many strands of life and poetry which these men wove into new English stuffs as durable as Ascham's broadcloth, and sometimes even more delightful.

When Elizabeth came to Cambridge in the August of that great year 1564, she saw in King's College Chapel a comedy by Plautus, a Latin 'Dido,' and an English scriptural play, *Ezechias,* by Mr. Udall. On a fourth night she was to have seen the *Ajax,* but she did not stay for it. Some of the students followed her to Hinchenbrook, and earned her grave displeasure by enacting there a tasteless, tactless 'show' about the imprisoned bishops: an omen full of promise for lovers of the stage; not so good for Spanish ambassadors, perhaps, or even for worthy Protestant professors who held that drama ought to be the handmaid of divinity.[90]

These performances, in Latin, Greek and English, were regular academic exercises, not reserved for great occasions like the royal visit. At Christ Church, from 1554 onwards, the rule was that a tragedy in Greek and one in Latin, besides a Greek and Latin comedy, should be given every year. At Cambridge we may recall with pride the testimony of Mr. William Soone who wrote in 1575 that if Euripides and Sophocles . . could have seen their plays as acted here, they would have thought even their Athens by comparison tedious. Oxford can reply that in 1605 the *Ajax* was acted there before King James with unparalleled splendour, the hero magnificent 'in a flowered gown and an ample wig.'

In the long list of these academic plays, which Peele and Marlowe must have seen when they were reading Greek at the Universities, some titles are particularly interesting — Dr. Legge's *Ricardus Tertius,* at Cambridge, Eade's *Julius Caesar* at Oxford. One of the earliest classical plays in English was a *Cambyses,* by Thomas Preston, the young Kingsman who had won the Queen's heart by his acting of Dido. It is poor creeping stuff, but the medley of metres and the mixture of crude comic stuff with the grave story from Herodotus is promising.

That Peele and Marlowe were directly influenced by Greek tragedy, no reasonable doubt is possible. Peele, we know, translated one of the Iphigeneia plays into English — and would have done more such work, had he not been idle, or rather 'of the poetical disposition, never to write so long as his money lasted.' He admired Thomas Watson's 'sad Antigone.' He had read Aeschylus for himself, if I am not mistaken. Witness this, from the magnificent prologue to *The Arraignment of Paris:*

King Priam's palace waste with flaming fire
Whose thick and foggy smoke, piercing the sky,
Must serve for messengers of sacrifice,

and this, of Ellen, in *Edward I:*

Ellen . . Hell in thy name, but Heaven in thy looks,

and this, from the same play:

The ground is all too base
For Eleanor to honour with her steps. . .

With the sequel, the 'fair tapestry,' the 'costly arras points.' The dreadful scene in which Eleanor makes the Mayoress nurse the adders — 'Draw forth her breast, and let the serpent suck its fill. Why so, now she is a nurse: suck on, sweet babe' — was suggested partly by Clytaemnestra's dream that she suckled a snake. It is a link between that and Shakespeare's Cleopatra — 'Dost thou not see my baby at my breast, that sucks the nurse asleep?'

But Peele's talent was lyrical, not dramatic. Marlowe created English heroic tragedy. Like Aeschylus he peopled a vast imaginative world with giants. Like Aeschylus, he needed, and he found, a great and thundering speech. No jigging veins of rhyming mother wits would serve, because this new world of imagination is a high astounding world. Inevitably we think of Aeschylus as the curtain rises on *Tamburlaine* and Cosroe begins:

> *Unhappy Persia, that in former age*
> *Hast been the seat of mighty conquerors. . .*

We seem to hear Darius again, mourning over Xerxes. Tamburlaine conquers Persia by Cosroe's treachery, and promises him the crown. But he means to wear it himself, 'and ride in triumph through Persepolis.'

> *Is it not passing brave to be a King?*
> *A god is not so glorious. . .*

Cosroe curses Tamburlaine, and dies. Tamburlaine puts on the crown amid the plaudits of the Persian traitors, boasting:

Not all the curses which the Furies breathe
Shall make me leave so rich a prize. . .

This pageant of a world delivered over to the Scourge of God, reminds us that, for Aeschylus, plague and famine are the two thongs of the double scourge of Ares. The accumulation of high-sounding names, Persepolis, Ecbatana, Trebizond, has a counterpart in the vast lyrical panorama of the *Persae,* where the peoples of the earth, bowmen, horsemen, savages in wild accoutrements, princes and nobles luxuriously arrayed, gather and break like a waterflood on the Greeks. But the King of Kings, the demi-god to whom Persia did obeisance, 'Xerxes, son of Darius, driver of the Assyrian car, in whose dragon-eyes there is a glint of steel,' is a puny mortal, a mere foil for the tragedy of his Empire. Tamburlaine is a hero at grips with destiny. As he moves from triumph to triumph, from cruelty to cruelty, his daemonic energy, his superb imagination, his passion for Zenocrate and his defiance of the last unconquerable enemy Death, make him tragic like Prometheus, Clytaemnestra, Ajax. Xerxes drove his Assyrian car to ruin, Phaëthon set the world aflame, when he drove the chariot of the Sun. The chariot of Tamburlaine's triumph, drawn by the Kings of Asia, becomes the symbol both of his greatness and of his impending death. When he resigns it in the end to his son, it has become significant, like the flood in the *Persae,* the net of Ruin in the *Oresteia.*

The reminiscences in *Faustus* are less apparent. But the *Hubris* which attempts the intellectual conquest of the universe, and will sell the soul for knowledge of heaven and hell, is a child begotten by the spirit of Greek Tragedy from mediaeval mysteries. The last temptation to which Faustus yields is Helen. Homer was her creator; but it was Aeschylus, in the *Agamemnon,* who changed her into a subtle, all-enchanting, all-destroying Spirit of Temptation.

It is now generally admitted that Shakespeare's 'small Latin' was by no means contemptible.[91] His Ovidian reminiscences are not all crumbs from the translator's table. Hecate's 'vaporous drop' on the corner of the moon comes to Shakespeare straight from Ovid, not from Golding. Ovid very probably got it from Sophocles, his *Magic-Root-Cutters,* a Medea play, from which Virgil also drew touches for Dido. So, when young Lucius reads his *Metamorphoses*, the book his mother gave him, he finds there the story of Tereus' treason and of Philomel's tragedy: it is a tale from Sophocles, whose *Tereus* was a great success, and gave Aristophanes the idea for his *Birds*. The tracking of such indirect allusions has its fascination.

What of the proverbial 'less Greek'? Ben Jonson, who made the phrase, was a man of solid learning. He need not have meant 'no Greek at all.' But we really have no evidence. When we search, with the late Mr. Churton Collins, for parallel passages, we find many. But the atmosphere was charged with the old stories and familiar commonplaces. When we have made deductions for all possible reminiscences of academic plays, Latin, Italian and French versions and adaptations, Ovid, Seneca and Plutarch, and the poet's talks — for he must have talked — with university wits and scholars, there is not much room left for direct and conscious borrowing. There are echoes of the *Ajax*. It would be surprising if there were not. There are very few echoes of Aeschylus. If Shakespeare really knew Greek at all well, that is even more surprising.

On the whole, the probability seems to be that he knew Sophocles in Latin and French versions, and did not know Aeschylus at all. His imaginative kinship with Aeschylus remains a fact of more importance than the trivialities of his indebtedness to Garnier and Seneca.

For instance, the nurse-type, in tragedy and comedy, had become a part of the world's literary stock-in-trade. As Mr. Lucas says: 'the nurse-confidante of the *Medea* and *Hippolytus* may be distantly related through Seneca to the greatest of her kind,' that is, to Juliet's nurse.[92] Yet in all drama there is only one nurse worthy of comparison with Juliet's. It is Orestes' nurse in the *Eumenides*. The Euripidean, Senecan ghosts, were no doubt the ancestors of many vengeful spirits. But the ghosts of Banquo and of Hamlet's father are still new creations, and there is no ghost in all the modern stage so majestic as Darius in the *Persae*, so tragic as Clytaemnestra in the *Oresteia*. Seneca's mad Hercules may have bred a Hieronimo and a Tilburina. Shakespeare created Ophelia: Aeschylus created Io. Pity, not anger, moves the Aeschylean Chorus, when they see and hear Cassandra: and in *Troilus,* when Cassandra's voice rings through the corridors of Priam's palace, do not 'these strains of divination work some touches of remorse?'

All we can assert with confidence — and it is worth asserting — is that Shakespeare's general conception of Tragedy owes much to the Greek masters, less through Seneca than through the nobler tradition of Plutarch, for example. That is why in *Antony and Cleopatra* Antony can moralize in the tone and almost in the phrases of Aeschylus:

> *When we in our viciousness grow hard,*
> *O misery on't, the wise gods seal our eyes,*
> *In our own filth drop our clear judgments, make us*
> *Adore our errors, laugh at us, while we strut*
> *To our confusion.*

Macbeth, perhaps, best illustrates the kinship of ideas. The Weird Sisters are the offspring of Shakespeare's genius, working freely on a mass of Greek and mediaeval notions. They are hags and witches such as King James persecuted in contemporary Scotland.[93] They are also the descendants of the Aeschylean Furies, and akin to that incarnate Temptation, that divine Apate, which, in Aeschylus, fawns on men until they fall in love with ruin. 'Oftentimes,' as Banquo says,

> *to win us to our harms,*
> *The instruments of darkness tell us truths,*
> *Win us with honest trifles.*

As the Chorus sing in the *Antigone:* 'Foul seems sometimes fair to him whom a god is leading from the straight way, into destruction.' So, with that old Greek commonplace, the Witches' Prelude finds its climax:

> *Fair is foul and foul is fair;*
> *Hover through the fog and filthy air.*

That strikes the first note of a recurrent tragic theme. The quiet interlude, in which the honest sergeant tells King Duncan of the hero's prowess, is essential to the drama. It ensures our interest in Macbeth, when he appears in person. In tone and colour it is deliberately contrasted with the Prelude and with the powerful effects which follow. But one sinister hint of tragic irony stands out:

> *So from that spring whence comfort seem'd to come*
> *Discomfort swells.*

It is driven home and made significant by the insistent phrase, 'Mark, King of Scotland, mark!'

After the interlude, the witches reappear. The sailor's wife, we know, was a poor woman of contemporary Edinburgh. But the sailor's fate is described in a phrase used by Aeschylean Furies two thousand years before King James was born: 'I'll drain him dry. . . He shall dwindle, peak and pine.' The Aeschylean Furies too were 'posters over sea and land.'

Macbeth and Banquo enter, in the storm. Macbeth's first words repeat the theme of the Witch-Prelude. The effect is exactly like the effect of an Aeschylean, Sophoclean repetition. 'So foul and fair a day I have not seen.' Again, after the three-fold Hail, Banquo exclaims:

Good sir, why do you start and seem to fear
Things that do seem so fair?

When the witches have gone, the development of this theme is Aeschylean even in its imagery:

This supernatural soliciting
Cannot be ill, cannot be good. . .
If good, why do I yield to that suggestion
Whose horrid image doth unfix my hair
And make my seated heart knock at my ribs
Against the use of nature?

So smiling Apate, with a first gleam of success,

entices men into ambition, covetousness, violence and ruin. 'Old Hubris breeds new Hubris, Sin breeds Sin,' said Aeschylus. 'Things bad begun make themselves strong by ill,' says Shakespeare's hero. 'It will have blood. They say, blood will have blood.' So said the Aeschylean Chorus.

Once more, there is nothing to prove conscious borrowing or direct acquaintance with the Greek originals. Everyone in the Renaissance had access to this common stock. In Shakespeare the old notions live again, and move us as they do in Aeschylus and Sophocles.

VII. THE STRASBOURG PLAYS

IN THE crude, cheerful dawn of the German Renaissance Greek Tragedy played a part. Melanchthon held that an unlettered theologian tried to fly without wings. He taught his pupils — many of them poor children whom he housed and fed — on Luther's principle, that young people should be free and learn from experience, not be kept in monkish seclusion from the world. Poetry, he thought, is the nurse of eloquence; so he practised turning Greek verse into Latin, though he confessed: 'I am a poor poet.' At meals, the scholar who had written the best verses, was crowned with ivy, and presided, with the title 'rex poeticus.' The acting of classical plays, the *Thyestes* of Seneca, the *Hecuba* in Erasmus' version, was a natural corollary. At the University of Wittenberg Melanchthon lectured on the *Antigone*, though he feared the barbarism of the age might make the attendance small. In 1534 he writes to Camerarius that 'in these stormy days' the reading of Sophocles gives him 'incredible pleasure.' 'No one can be so made of iron as to read of Jocasta's end without emotion. . . I myself often at the mere reading shudder all over.' Obviously this is an aesthetic appreciation. Yet he expressly says that tragedies are to be read not for pleasure, but for moral edification.[94]

The stormy days continued, but the work went on. Veit Oertel of Winsheim, Melanchthon's pupil and deputy at Wittenberg, translated the whole of Sophocles into Latin. An address which he delivered on Greek Tragedy in 1548 well illustrates the moral and religious twist which a Protestant German teacher naturally gives the theme. He began with praise to God for the scheme of man's salvation, and particularly for His mercy to Wittenberg. The schools, now happily reopened after a time of war, were 'a chorus of the arts' to praise Him. The students return to their hive and their honey-making: let them take a lesson from Virgil's bees, and from the crocus, which, as Pliny said, grows more abundantly if it be trampled under foot. Euripides is difficult, but, as Ovid said, a rich soil tires the oxen, but the labour giveth delight. What advantage is there in the study of Greek Tragedy? ‘First, as life without true piety is itself an horrible and wretched tragedy, so the written plays are a picture of our miserable life, or rather of the errors, wickednesses, crimes, with which it is infested, as well as of the punishments which flood upon the human race like a sea of troubles, yet are insufficient to abate our lusts. The reading of tragedies is, as it were, a theatre, in which we see the ways and minds of men, the memorials of events, chances, counsels, good and bad success, rewards of virtue, punishment of crime, set forth to view and exampled in illustrious persons, that they may more strongly move, more sharply stimulate.’ ‘Not if I had an hundred tongues,’ he cries, ‘could I expound the fullness of this theme. . .’ ‘This is the urgent refrain, the repeated lesson of the tragedians, that God is, that He cares for human things, that men are not born by chance, that events flow not at random, but that all is divinely governed. When Satan plunged the world in darkness after our first parents fell, he tried to bring back chaos. But God raised up poets, men of genius, to keep truth alive. To a corrupt and gluttonous age, Greek tragedy still preaches Virgil's lesson,

"Discite justitiam moniti, et non temnere divos." If men will not listen, we must sing, like Orpheus, to the stones and trees. The enemies of learning may mock us and oppress us; but we will not leave our post of duty. God and the commonwealth demand our loyalty. Listen to these dead teachers, if you will not heed the living.'

When Winsheim made this eloquent appeal at Wittenberg, John Sturm had been teaching some ten years at Strasbourg. From his work sprang that famous University, and, as a by-product, a remarkable theatrical development. School recitals led to public performances, and before Sturm retired, in 1581, the academic theatre of Strasbourg had become a public institution of which Alsace was proud. Presently there came travelling companies, Italian and French, and, at the end of the century, English players. In the Court of the University, once a Dominican Monastery, scriptural and classical plays were acted to large audiences. Students and teachers took part. The city police kept order and the city trumpeters helped with the music.[95]

Among the plays performed were the *Ajax*, in 1587 and 1608, in Latin, and, in 1609, the

Prometheus, in Greek. To make the plays intelligible to all, a Prologue explained the story, and an Epilogue the moral, and the audience was given a German book of words. Where a Messenger's speech described some exciting event, a new scene, specially composed for the occasion, enacted it as well. Pageantry, dancing and music were lavishly provided, and the result must have been a lively entertainment, shocking perhaps to pedantry, but full of hope for those who think that learning is a servant of the arts. Spangenberg, a printer's corrector, a theological student, and a man of genius, was the life and soul of these delightful shows from 1591 to 1611. He wrote the German versions which we still possess.

The *Ajax* began with a prologue by Perfidy. She explains that she is much honoured at Court, where she is known as Foresight, and her followers are called Worldly-Wise. The scene is arranged on the mediaeval multiple principle, with houses for the Greek and Trojan camps, a Temple and a neutral field. Truce is proclaimed between the armies. Paris and Deïphobus concoct a plot against Achilles, and entice him to the temple on the pretext that King Priam is inclined to favour his suit for the

Trojan princess Polyxena. A Greek soldier sees him going, and informs Ulysses, Diomed and Ajax. They arrive too late, but they see the murderers of Achilles running away in sudden panic to their camp. Ulysses goes for help. Ajax shoulders the body of his friend, and carries it homeward. But Perfidy incites the Trojans to return. A fight ensues. The Greeks are winning. Perfidy brings up the Amazons on the Trojan side. 'Lass nicht ab,' she screams, 'Biss dass dein Grimm verderbet hab Zu grund das ganz menschlich Geschlecht.' It is an excellent climax. First this Fury whispered her suggestions to Deïphobus and Paris: then she roused the Trojans: now she eggs on the whole multitude.

In the battle, the Greeks win. Then Ajax and Odysseus quarrel, and Agamemnon intervenes. The second act consists of the trial, with long speeches, and a fine monologue by Ajax, madly threatening his enemies after the verdict. The character of Ajax here is Sophoclean, and the contrast with the sympathetic Ulysses is well sustained.

After that we come to Sophocles. A dumb show of the mad Ajax adds a comic effect of horseplay with the ram. The arrival of the

Chorus is the signal for fresh novelties. Four sailors recite the Latin anapaests, but a singing chorus follows, introducing Diana and the Eumenides, 'that is, raging hellish women of night,' who shake their snaky locks when the Chorus pray for pity. In 1587 the image of Diana was surrounded by dancers, grouped 'in the shape of a rose': and the Salamis ode was accompanied by a pageant of two circles, 'like a moon,' one formed of Salaminians praising Apollo, the other of Satyrs dancing to Pan. Again, the emotion of the Chorus was symbolized by a tableau 'in the shape of a heart with a cross in the centre' — that is, Ajax pierced by the sword. In 1608 these delights were modified, but there were still a singing Chorus of satyrs and forest-gods and a Hymn to Happiness. At the end, an elaborate ritual, with offerings of 'salt, fruit, blood, wine, milk and oil,' recalled with modern effects the ancient cult of the dead. What could be more charming, in its mixture of old and new, than the lament of Eurysakes:

> *Aber Hertzliebster Vatter mein*
> *Der du jetzt nunmehr wohnest fein*
> *In dem Elysischen Lustgarten. . .*

Nimm an dem letzten Dienst gewiss
Deins lieben Sohns Eurysakis,
Und ruhe sanfft. . . ?

In the *Prometheus,* a new first act presented the hero giving fire to men, men worshipping him, and Zeus intervening, furious. Then followed the Aeschylean play. These pageant-lovers must have enjoyed the Nymphs and Neptune. The central tableau was enlivened with a charming Morality, Apollo and the Muses with the gifts of the Free Arts on one side, on the other Pleasure with the seductive Vices. The young people had to choose. Apollo promised good students that they should be churchmen, statesmen, doctors and judges. Pleasure distributed her prizes, a horse's neck for the horsey youth, a monkey's head for the lad who courts popularity, a pig's head for the drunkard, and a donkey's head for the slug-a-bed. So back to the play. An extra scene represents the jealous Juno, wakeful Argus lulled to sleep by Mercury's piping, and Io driven mad. Then Aeschylus again.

Epilogues point the moral. Sophocles would not have objected to the edifying sentiment which closes the *Ajax* — 'We should be placable and forgive our enemies, especially after death.' Aeschylus might have been surprised, but hardly annoyed, to learn that his play teaches duty and gratitude to God. Learned men are sent to teach us 'God's word, worldly policy and household management.' Let us be grateful. Prometheus did not invent the fire, but brought it from heaven. He had to suffer in order to help us: that is, wicked, jealous people cannot bear to see the world go right, and persecute wise teachers. Jupiter is a type of tyranny, like the Emperor Julian, who would not let the Christians learn the arts. Could it be worse in Turkey? Let us be thankful for good rulers. Finally, the play shows the strength of a good conscience, and the way of the world, which runs after vanities. God gave Germany her Prometheus — the inventor of the printing-press. See how it can be used, and how, alas, often it is abused.

The perfidy and tyranny of war destroyed many flowers of poetry in Germany before Spangenberg's generation came to an end. Nearly two centuries passed before the singing-Chorus took up again the praise of Apollo and the free arts.

VIII. MILTON

'RHUBARB and sugarcandie, the pleasant and the profitable'[96] are the gifts of poetry according to Sir John Harington. And, in spite of Parnassians, it is no bad working definition. When Puritans declaim against the theatre it is well that Tragedy can answer 'Teachers best Of moral prudence, with delight received, In brief sententious precepts.' It is a dangerous defence, of course. For sheer weight of moralizing Seneca will tip the scale against Aeschylus, to say nothing of Sophocles or Shakespeare. Still, as Aristotle urged in answer to the Puritan Plato, one effect of a good tragedy may be not merely to excite emotion, but to rid and purge us of its tyranny by means of fear and pity. Or, as an excellent Elizabethan critic puts it, the effect may be 'the redress of boistrous and sturdy courages by Persuasion, the consolation and repose of temperate minds . . the common solace of mankind in all the travails . . of this transitory life.'[97]

Such was the argument which made it possible for Milton to approve the theatre — at least if Jonson's learned sock be on, or Shakespeare warble his native woodnotes. Jonson's Comedy has the ancient gravity of purpose, and Shakespeare's music is a bird-song, part of nature's chorus to God. Pensive Melancholy too may sometimes leave the dim religious light of the cloister, to sit, no less religiously bemused, while gorgeous Tragedy sweeps by. All his life Milton cherished the hope that he might add his contribution to the little heap of 'what, though rare, of later age ennobled hath the buskin'd stage,' and his early works, as well as *Samson,* his last masterpiece, reveal his love of the Greek drama. Aeschylus is one begetter of his full-mouthed harmonies in prose. His vision of a noble nation, nurtured in liberty by learning, mounting like an eagle, mewing her mighty youth, is in part Hebraic, but in part Greek. The exultation in his voice when he talks of freedom, and his images, copious and closely pressed and elaborately developed, mark his kinship with Aeschylus. No reader of the *Prometheus* can doubt that Aeschylus has fired the English poet's imagination, and given him wings to soar 'above the Aonian mount' and find in the debate of Heaven and Hell an argument which far transcends the bickering of Homer's Zeus and Hera. Lucifer is Aeschylean, not only through the conception of his tragic greatness, but by the art with which that greatness is revealed in image after image, cunningly arranged: first, when we see him prostrate, after his fall from heaven, like Leviathan, by whose mountainous side a whaler's skiff is moored; the image is framed by two references to the battles of the gods and giants: then upright — the picture framed by two gracious Italian sketches — grasping his spear, which is like the mast of a Norwegian ship. When he spreads his wings for the adventure against man, he sets out and reaches port like a ship with outspread sails. And when at last, after the horrors of chaos, the sweet airs of Paradise greet him, they are like the fragrant odours of a fleet of merchantmen, plying with precious spices in far seas.[98] That use of a sustained, repeated image, is Aeschylean.

In *Paradise Regained* the panegyric of Athens is unfortunately spoken by the Tempter, but is none the less eloquent for that. Against Christ's answer, which is more sophistical than Christian, we can put the Saviour's gentle meditation at the beginning of the work. He, who could violently overcome all enemies, and put down tyranny by tyranny, holds it more humane, more heavenly, first:

> *By winning words to conquer willing hearts*
> *And make Persuasion do the work of Fear.*[99]

He will try to teach the erring soul, 'the stubborn only to subdue.' The last phrase is an echo of Virgil's *parcere subiectis et debellare superbos.* But it was Athena in the *Eumenides* who, to end a tale of sin and hate, won willing hearts by words, and did the work of Fear by sweet Persuasion. So Milton links his vision of redeeming Love with the Aeschylean thought of saving Wisdom. Nor is Sophocles left without a tribute. When the Tempter offers Christ an earthly crown, he quotes the words of Oedipus to Creon:

> *What followers, what retinue canst thou gain. . . ?*
> *Money brings honour, friends, conquest and realms.*[100]

Christ's answer, with its picture of a true King, serving his people, governing his own passions, links Milton's Christian ideal again with thoughts of Sophocles and Virgil.

On some aspects of theology and social theory, *Samson Agonistes* is more primitive and less religious than the ' fabulous imaginations ' of the Athenian poets. But the grim theology makes excellent drama. We accept as tragic symbols, the God of Israel and the Dagon of the Philistines. We enlist with Samson in the cause of God against evil. With him we feel our spirits droop when God seems to withdraw His guidance: with him we summon energy to resist temptation — for Dalila is indeed a temptress, not to be denied without passion: with him we challenge Harapha, and find that, after all, God is still with us, calling us to the festival of Dagon, which shall be God's triumph, though we die. Then, with Manoah, we live through the tragedy again, and conclude that, at the heart of life, there may be found, not tears and wailing merely, but peace and consolation — calm of mind, all passion spent.

The dramatic theme is the recovery of a Christian soul after great sin. Such recovery, Milton holds, is made possible only by the Grace of God, and through the Christian's own heroic effort. The process is — admission of full undivided guilt, renunciation of the pleasant evil which has caused the fall, and, lastly, when strength returns, obedience to God's call. When light is re-kindled in the soul, the way to life is still through death. Samson wins back his glory as Israel's champion, but must give his life, a willing, happy sacrifice.

It has been said, not truly, that the play lacks action. The action takes place in the hero's soul. His emotions are expressed in eloquence of word and gesture, and only rarely, but with all the more effect, in isolated and emphatic physical movement. The play belongs to the same class (it is sometimes called 'static' drama) as the *Prometheus* and the *Oedipus at Colonus*. To both these heroes, indeed, Milton intends us to observe a likeness and a contrast. Prometheus, strong in his good cause, though physically tortured, rejects the kindly offices of Ocean, pities Io, resists the threats of Hermes, and defies the storm. Oedipus, blind and scorned, but conscious that his evils have been his afflictions rather than his crimes, rejects the offers of the treacherous Thebans and, as he denounces them, grows confident in a belief that he is marked out by the gods for honour: at last, he hears the call of Zeus and goes to a death which is a triumph.

Samson, blind, scorned, imprisoned, by contrition, self-examination and confession gains self-knowledge, which, although at first it overwhelms him, is the condition of recovery. This first part ends in weariness and a prayer for death. The second part consists of two great scenes, the renunciation of Dalila and the challenge to Harapha. Through the renunciation Samson gains strength for the challenge, and the movement ends with his reply to the foreboding of the Chorus: 'If they kill me, I shall welcome death. But it may be that, with my death, they may draw ruin on themselves.' The third part begins with the demand of the Philistine Messenger that Samson should attend the festival of Dagon. He refuses; then he hears the call and goes. It ends with Manoah, and the story of the hero's death and vindication.

This formal, balanced scheme, is Greek. Milton is using the technique which he has learnt from Aeschylus and Sophocles, and which they learnt from Homer and from music. He knows the tradition well — 'Aeolian charms and Dorian lyric odes. And his who gave them breath, but higher sung . . Homer. . . Thence what the lofty grave tragedians taught.'

The theme of the first movement, then, is a confession and humiliation, not without hints of hope. After each act of confession there comes a gleam of light, followed — as anyone may understand from Bunyan's allegory, if not from experience, — by a relapse into despondency. Analysis reveals the Aeschylean symmetry of the workmanship.

A *little onward lend thy guiding hand*
T*o these dark steps, a little further on,*
F*or yonder bank gives choice of sun and shade.*

So the first paragraph begins. It ends with a balancing imperative, 'Leave me. Here let me respire.' At the beginning is 'the choice of sun and shade'; at the end, 'the breath of heaven, with dayspring born.' At the centre, contrasted with God's air and sunlight, is the dank air of prison.

The second paragraph begins with Dagon's day of festival, and ends with God's dayspring — 'Light, the prime work of God. . .' At the centre are two contrasted figures — Samson, 'Eyeless, in Gaza, at the mill, with slaves, myself in bonds,' and 'the woman' who betrayed him. And framing this central picture are two balanced instances of the thoughts which, at this stage of the soul's drama, sting, like hornets — Why did God choose him, foretell his birth by angel messengers, and have him reared apart from ordinary men, if this was to be the end? And why did God give strength without a corresponding gift of wisdom?

This is the pattern:

Guide me onward . . blind . . yonder is choice of sun and shade.
Contrast: the dank air of prison.
The breath of Heaven, with dayspring born. . . Here leave me to respire.

Dagon's festal day . . ease for the body . . but the mind beset by hornets.
Why did God choose me . . for this?
To be a blind slave . . by my own fault . . I fell to the Woman, . .
But why did God give me strength without wisdom? Question not God.
Light, the prime work of God . . total eclipse without all hope of day.

Then the noble epode, or after-song, reinforcing the main theme:

O first created beam, and Thou, great Word, Let there be Light. . .

My *darkness and silence . . no light or life in the soul . . this living death . . myself my sepulchre. . .*
And *with this worst evil, no relief from the other, ordinary evils of captivity among enemies.*

When Samson first appears, who can help thinking of Oedipus, led by Antigone to the grove of the Eumenides? When he cries to the Light, who can help remembering the cry of Prometheus: 'O thou, bright air of heaven, ye swift-winged breezes. . . ?' And yet how new is the effect. At the very centre of the whole scheme, in the second paragraph is the hero's first confession, 'By my own fault.'

These are the themes which the sequel musically develops. The Chorus find him 'lying at random, carelessly diffused, As by himself given over.' Their loyalty, he says, revives him. Blindness has now become his least affliction — he would be ashamed, if he could see them. But there are thoughts that sting worse than physical pain — Am I not sung for a fool? Why did God give strength without wisdom?

The answer is 'Tax not divine disposal. Wise men too have fallen.' But, they ask, what motive made him marry a Philistine woman? God, he answers, prompted him to marry the first treacherous wife, the woman of Timna, as a trick against the enemy. The second marriage he thought lawful for the same end. But the woman, though she betrayed him, was not the prime cause. He fell by his own fault.

The confession is the first step to recovery. The Chorus accept his explanation, though God's ways puzzle them. 'Samson was never found remiss against the enemy. Yet Israel still serves?' 'That fault I take not on me. . . Israel suffers for the treachery and ingratitude of her governors.' 'Yes, like Gideon and Jephtha, you have been neglected.' 'They may neglect me. . . They can not neglect God's deliverance.'

So faith revives after confession. Samson sees hope for Israel, none yet for himself.

The Chorus brood on the moral mystery. Just are the ways of God: some think there is no God: but they are fools and few: more doubt His justice. His ways seem to contradict his own decrees. He only can dispense with His own laws — for proof, this prompting of the Nazarite to marry the fallacious bride. . .

So, in the first ode of the *Agamemnon*, the Chorus brood on the just, harsh ways of Zeus.

But what are we to think of this solution? It is dramatic. The sequel shows that it is not the whole, at any rate, of Milton's theory.

It is the turn of Samson's father to complain. Why did God grant my prayer for a son? Why did the angel prophesy a hero? Why was he nurtured as a plant select for God? 'Appoint not heavenly disposition. I was the sole cause. . . It is just.' The Timna woman, Samson now thinks, was meant by God as a warning. He ought to have learnt his lesson. Three assaults from Dalila he resisted: then he fell. His own effeminacy made him her slave, and that slavery was worse than his present bondage. Manoah doubts — and so, of course, does Milton — whether God really prompted the affair with the woman of Timna. 'I only know it was the first time that the Philistines triumphed. . . Well, you sinned, and you have paid more than enough. But the worst comes to-day. Dagon's triumph is due to you.' 'That is true. I have brought pomp to Dagon, and dishonour to God. That is my worst affliction.'

Not blindness, nor the humiliation of being sung as a fool, nor the bitter question why God deals with him thus — only the dishonour he has brought to God. As always, the new stage in self-knowledge brings hope. 'It is now God against Dagon. God will arise.'

Manoah accepts the prophecy, and explains his plan for a ransom. 'No, I betrayed God's secret. I must suffer.' 'Leave the punishment to God. Do not afflict yourself. He may grant you freedom and life.' 'I ask for pardon, not for life.' So, in spite of the consolations of the Chorus and Manoah, Samson falls into complete despondency. His spiritual torment rankles and festers: his remorse is armed with stings. He is hopeless. His one prayer is for death.

The first movement is ended. The Chorus sing. All ordinary comforts of wisdom are of no avail, unless there be some secret source from within, nay, from above. The ways of God are strange.

Enter Dalila, sumptuously beautiful, in tears; a creature of impulse, still attracted by Samson, anxious to excuse herself. For him she is incarnate Temptation.

There are three assaults of argument, each repelled — not without pain. Then her sudden movement, 'Let me at least touch you,' and his cry of anguish, 'Not for thy life! . . At distance I forgive you. . .' She is too shallow to understand 'the inward passion, the secret sting of amorous remorse.' She relapses to her old lightness. She will turn to her own people. They will honour her. So she leaves him, 'a serpent, shown at the end by the sting.'

The brooding of the Chorus on the mystery of women, their inconstancy, their charm, their ruinous effects, is, of course, inspired by memories of the Helen-Clytaemnestra Chorus in the *Agamemnon.*

Then comes Harapha, arrogant and strong. The hero's growing strength, the pent-up energy, so painfully controlled in the last scene, find an outlet. Three times he challenges the Philistine to single combat; then, with sudden violence, rises, as to fight him. Harapha flies. The Chorus fear he will rouse the Philistines to fresh outrage. 'If they kill me, death is welcome.' Samson answers: 'But, with my death, perhaps, they will draw upon themselves their own destruction.'

Samson is ready for the summons to Dagon's festival. He refuses. His new strength must be used for God. When the Messenger has gone, he feels the prompting of the Spirit. He sees and welcomes his task. He goes, amid the prayers of the Chorus, who have not understood. They are like the followers of Ajax, when he went to settle his account with heaven.

Manoah's touching story of his efforts and his hopes is interrupted, first by the Philistine shout of triumph, then by the hideous noise of ruin. The Hebrew Messenger brings news of the catastrophe, and Manoah speaks the final word of comfort:

> H*is servants He with new acquist*
> O*f true experience from this great event*
> I*n peace and consolation hath dismissed*
> W*ith calm of mind, all passion spent.*

It is the closing harmony which at length resolves the discord — 'Ease to the body some, none to the mind.'

IX. NEO-CLASSICS AND ROMANTICS

WHEN Milton died, in 1674, French Classical Tragedy was in full splendour. *Andromaque* was produced in 1667, *Phèdre* in 1677. Dryden's *All for Love* was produced in the same year.

In France, after Jodelle's brilliant beginning, there had been a time of academic reaction, corresponding with the gloomy days of civil and religious struggle. Grévin, in 1562, led the way back from Greek to Seneca, and began the dreary talk about dramatic rules and 'Unities.' Garnier's *Antigone* took incidents from Sophocles as part of its material but the result was frigid, mechanical, insincere.

Scaliger's *Poetics* appeared in 1561, and his theories—or the theories attributed to him, for he, like Aristotle, was made responsible for much more than he said—henceforward played a great part both for good and evil in French criticism. He was not the first Italian critic—

Cinthio, the Senecan adaptor, had preceded him — who deduced imaginary ' rules ' from the supposed perfection — often much misunderstood — of Virgil and of Seneca. These rules they attributed to Aristotle, twisting his obvious meaning when it did not fit their theory. Then they applied them as a test to Homer and Sophocles. To their astonishment and patriotic satisfaction, they found that the Greek writers either did not know or did not follow ' the rules.' The inference was obvious. Virgil and Seneca, on Aristotle's own showing, were greater artists than the Greeks themselves.

The effect on the criticism of epic has been serious. The discovery of Homer's ' improprieties ' led directly, in the Abbé d'Aubignac's admirably ordered system, to the inference that, since Homer certainly was the prince of poets, he could not possibly have written anything so ' incorrect ' as our present *Iliad.* Happily, but surprisingly, d'Aubignac, when he came to test the *Ajax* by the rules, contrived to find a verdict for the defendant. Corneille was less fortunate.

As a matter of fact the Unities were neither observed by the Greeks nor advocated by Aristotle, nor even imposed as rigid laws by Scaliger himself. Nevertheless, they served a useful purpose. They provided Racine with a set of conventions, exactly suited to his genius. So he exploited them, from no slavish sense of duty to the ancients, but because they served his turn. The concentration of the tragic action in one place and one short period of time became in his hands a perfectly legitimate device for securing the utmost poignancy of effect. His stately rhetoric, his rigid, 'artificial' forms, his much abused sub-plots and 'confidantes,' are means to the same end: the representation of great human spirits, highly intelligent and acutely sensitive, caught, struggling, overwhelmed in growing, masterful, and finally destructive passions.

He admired Euripides, and reinterpreted many of his themes. But his artistic affinity was with Sophocles. In a well known letter Valincour recalls a day at Auteuil when Racine declaimed the whole *Oedipus Tyrannus* to a company of friends, translating as he went along.[101] Fénelon says that Racine once had an idea of writing an *Oedipus* himself, excluding love-intrigue and keeping Greek simplicity. Certainly he much admired and studied the play. Joad's cry in *Athalie,*

Voilà donc quels vengeurs s'arment pour ta querelle!
Des prêtres, des enfants!

is a fine echo of the first scene. So is the first line of Esther: 'De l'antique Jacob jeune posterité.' More remarkable than such reminiscences is the technical affinity. Only Racine and Sophocles have created a dramatic diction rigorously stripped of ornament, yet never commonplace, flexible, logical and lucid, and above all more vivid than the language of real life, revealing at every moment, behind the speaker's mask of dignity, the stress of passion and the play of thought. They are alike too in their constructive talent. Each cuts away irrelevance, and uses a severe economy of means to clarify and heighten the dramatic issues. Each is a master of crescendo and diminuendo, and weaves a complicated chain of incidents into a plot theatrically simple and effective. The differences, of course, are important too. Racine was a courtier and a Christian: Sophocles was neither. Sophocles had no curtain, and preferred (as a rule: the *Electra* is exceptional) a quiet close to a violent catastrophe. But in no drama except that of Sophocles and

Racine have a powerful imagination and a rich invention been so perfectly controlled by intellect.

In spite of many aberrations, the Parisian theatre has never lost touch with this great tradition of simplicity and dignity. The *Oedipus* is still better played, and Sophocles more understood, in France than anywhere else in the world. And in Italy, Alfieri, following Racine, made strong heroic plays. In England, though the influence was strongly felt, the theatrical results were melancholy. Still, there is passion and there is beauty in the tirades of Dryden's Cleopatra (in *All for Love*), though his work has never the formal strength of classical French Tragedy. As for Lee, his collaborator in the forgotten *Oedipus* (1679: everyone in those days, except Racine himself, tried his hand at the great theme), he knew and 'imitated' Sophocles more closely than Dryden; but his work is worthless, imitation without understanding. On the whole, in our so-called 'Classical age,' English audiences and writers had lost the sense of tragedy. We should like to have been present at the first performances of Addison's *Cato* (1723), Thomson's *Agamem-*

non (1738) and Dr. Johnson's *Irene* (1748), but for the sake of the actors and the audience, not for the play. We should like to have seen Quin as Agamemnon, Mrs. Porter as Clytaemnestra, Mrs. Cibber as Cassandra, to join in the applause which greeted Mr. Pope, and to watch Thomson in the gallery, punctuating Mrs. Cibber's periods with audible declamation. And again, from the pompous mouthing of *Irene,* we should turn with pleasure to the sight of Dr. Johnson, 'in a conspicuous side-box,' with his wig, new curled, his scarlet, gold-laced waistcoat, purchased for this evening, and his 'tranquil, majestic air.' But we should have been very far away from ancient Athens. It was no contemptible age. It did much to discover reasonable means of government and social intercourse. Common sense is not without its value. But our classical age was not inspired by Greece. It was Latin in many of its virtues and in its imaginative limitations.

Pope's *Iliad* was exceptional, and its popularity was full of promise for the future. Bentley might growl 'You must not call it Homer,' but there was more of Homer to be learnt from it than from the contemporary classical dons at the Universities. Consult, for instance, the

Homeric Gnomologia of the great Duport of Cambridge, a compendium, made for the benefit of 'young noblemen' and others, of the brief sententious maxims, which display the wisdom of the poet and the learning of the commentator. This medley of ancient maxims — with parallels from Scripture — together with some knowledge of the language, was the fare on which the students of the time were still nourished. The poetry, as poetry, was hardly offered them at all. Still, the light burnt, however feebly, in many a country parsonage.[102]

Fielding, who was a schoolboy when the great translation appeared, had a fresh and genuine appreciation of the ancient story-maker. The eulogy of the *Iliad* which he puts into the mouth of Parson Adams reflects his own enthusiasm. Aeschylus, of course, was the good man's hero. He had copied all the plays with his own hand — for he was poor, and books were expensive — and he carried the precious manuscript about with him on all his journeys. A passage of Aeschylus could 'entertain him for three miles together, without suffering him once to reflect on his fellow-traveller.' Once, in his absorption, he waded up to the waist through a filthy pond when, if he had looked over the hedge, he would have found a footpath. In a village, where he was arrested, his mysterious book aroused suspicion. The country Justice thought it a book in cypher. 'Aeschylus,' said the clerk, 'that is an outlandish name.' 'A fictitious name, rather, I believe,' said the Justice. Appeal was made to the village parson. But the Doctor said: 'It begins with the catechism in Greek.' 'Ay, ay,' said the parson. 'Polloki toi — what's your name?'

Parson Adams had not read Shakespeare, or any modern playwright except Addison. His admiration for Sophocles is conventional, and enlivened by Fielding's humour. Tekmessa's appeal to *Ajax,* he says, is less moving than Andromache's to Hector. 'Yet Sophocles was the greatest genius who ever wrote tragedy: nor have any of his successors in that way, that is to say, neither Euripides nor Seneca the tragedian, been able to come near him. As to his sentiments and diction, I need say nothing: the former are particularly remarkable for the utmost perfection in that head, namely propriety; and, as to the latter, Aristotle, whom doubtless you have read over and over, is very diffuse.' [103]

In 1759 appeared, with a dedication to the Prince of Wales, and a list of subscribers, including Horace Walpole ('2 copies'), the first complete English verse translation of Sophocles, by Francklin, Regius Professor of Greek at Cambridge. It was followed in 1777 by Potter's Aeschylus. Greek Tragedy, Francklin owns, is out of fashion: 'Homer, Xenophon and Demosthenes have of late years put on an English habit and gained admission into what is called polite company,' but the dramatists 'very seldom make their appearance, at least with dirty leaves, in the libraries of the great.' The fault is partly with the 'dull and phlegmatic commentators,' their 'verbal criticisms, various readings, or general and trite exclamations of undistinguishing applause': — a courageous outburst from a Cambridge Regius Professor.

Still, though no pedant, Francklin was an accurate scholar. His blank verse is by no means contemptible:

> I *had it not from Jove, nor the just gods*
> W*ho rule below; nor could I ever think*
> A *mortal's law of pow'r or strength sufficient*
> T*o abrogate th' unwritten law divine,*
> I*mmutable, eternal. . .*

He does not understand Aeschylus, whom he calls the Julio Romano of Greek drama, nor much like Euripides, whom he calls the Correggio. Sophocles, 'the Raphael,' is his man — elegant, noble, sublime, equal, unexceptionable. Unexceptionable, that is, as a rule. 'The ladies will probably be surprised, and, I doubt not, equally pleased, to meet, in so ancient a writer with an ode expressly on the power of Love.' When Chrysothemis comes running, actually running, with her good news, Francklin quotes uneasily Camerarius' comment: 'A lady should not run, *quoniam in mulieribus cunctabunda omnia magis probentur.*' Servants, too, in democratic Athens, sometimes addressed their masters with 'a familiarity which modern delicacy would scarcely admit.' But Francklin is Englishman enough to applaud Creon when he tells Oedipus that kings need not be obeyed if their orders are unjust.[104] 'This republican sentiment . . is but ill-suited to the taste of an arbitrary government. Mr. Dacier has, therefore, with the true spirit of a Frenchman, apologised in his notes for this freedom.'

In 1759, when this mild protest appeared, Burns and Schiller were born. Lessing was thirty years old, and Goethe ten. The Romantic revival and the French revolution were brewing. Both movements led poets back to Aeschylus. His faith in liberty, his optimism, his harmonies evolved through struggle out of chaos, made his work an inspiration not to Goethe only, but to Shelley, and in turn to Victor Hugo and to Swinburne. His vast conceptions, the rich variety of his images, his homeliness and majesty appealed to men who seemed to be discovering for the first time the mystery and glory of the sunrise and the mountain peaks and torrents, the infinite variety of nature and of man. There were bad reasons too for this romantic fashion. Scholars as well as laymen still imagined that the father of the drama was no artist. The complaint that Aeschylus was ' turgid, chaotic, irregular ' now became a compliment. It was not really deserved.

Landor, who was born in 1775, is said [105] to have been the first Oxford man to wear his own hair without powder. He recognized Aeschylus as the greatest of the Greek tragedians, a champion of liberty, with ' the loud clear challenge, the firm unstealthy step of an erect broad-chested soldier.' There is, indeed, no poet who better fulfils Landor's three conditions of poetic excellence, 'invention, energy, and grandeur of design.' At a performance of the *Prometheus* in ancient Athens Landor imagines the first meeting of Aspasia and Pericles.[106]

The choice of the *Prometheus* is significant. Every romantic poet at this time turned instinctively to the *Prometheus,* just as every would-be classicist had turned to the *Oedipus* a century earlier. Dacier thought the *Prometheus* 'a dramatic monstrosity': Fontenelle supposed its author must have been a 'sort of madman, with a lively imagination': Voltaire called it barbarous. Schlegel thought it a masterpiece. For him the gift of fire meant the gift of culture to mankind. Goethe conceived the hero as an image of himself — a prophet, reforming a bad world. Byron, of course, had no doubt that Prometheus symbolized a more interesting type of rebel. 'Of the *Prometheus* I was passionately fond as a boy. . . If not exactly in my plan, it has always been so much in my head that I can easily conceive its influence on all, or anything that I have ever written.' Swinburne and Meredith, later on, were to find in it an image for Italy, ' stretched on Promethean rocks, torn by fouler eagles.' The names of Rossetti, Longfellow, Mrs. Browning, Lowell, Robert Bridges, remind us of the amazing ever-renewed vitality of this great poem.

But Shelley was the greatest of them all. He read the *Prometheus* over and over again — once with Byron on the shores of Lake Leman. The best scenes of his own *Prometheus Unbound,* the dreams and visions of the early part, are exquisite developments of Aeschylean themes. His Prometheus, he says, is ' a Satan, exempt from the taints of ambition, envy, revenge, and a desire for personal aggrandisement.' His Zeus is the Jehovah of the Old Testament in darkest mood, as seen by a hater of priests and a believer in the perfectibility of man. Naturally Shelley felt averse ' from a catastrophe so feeble as that of reconciling the Champion with the Oppressor of mankind.' Aeschylus might have answered: ' In my universe, intelligence and love are not enough to inaugurate a reign of happiness: they have to make terms with brutal facts: in the long run, sometimes, they prove strong enough to make a favourable bargain.' Or he might have pointed, as an illustration of his meaning, to Shelley's echo of his work in *Hellas*.

The song of 'Greece and her foundations, built below the tide of war, Based on the crystalline sea Of thought . .' is interrupted by the noise of a falling Empire, the shrieks for Mercy, and the shouts of 'Kill! Kill! Kill!' Then comes a still small voice, thus:

Revenge and wrong bring forth their kind,
The foul cubs like their parents are,
Their den is in their guilty mind,
And conscience feeds them with despair.

In sacred Athens, near the fane
Of Wisdom, Pity's altar stood. . .[107]

The return to 'Sacred Athens' after the discordant interlude, and the image of the foul cubs, with its detailed development — the den the mind, the food despair — are Aeschylean. And the reference to Wisdom and Pity, though linked by Shelley with later associations, is meant to remind us that Pity and Wisdom are in fact the solution of the *Oresteia*. Did not pity joined with wisdom, perhaps, dictate the sequel to the *Prometheus Vinctus?* And, on

Shelley's own theory, does not the perfect hero, who defies power which seems omnipotent, also 'forgive wrongs blacker than death or night?'

Shelley also loved, and passionately studied, Sophocles. The *Cenci*[108] proves it. Beatrice, he says, is intended to be 'a gentle and amiable being . . thwarted from her nature by the necessity of circumstances and opinion. . . Revenge and retaliation are pernicious mistakes: Beatrice would have been wiser and better if she had thought this, but less tragic.' She is, in fact, like Electra in Sophocles. She says to the guests in the first act:

Oh think what deep wrongs must have blotted out
First love, then reverence in a child's pure mind
Till it thus vanquish shame and fear. . .

So Electra cries: 'I am ashamed. But in such wrongs, neither piety nor modesty is possible.'

There are many touches of reminiscence. This violent image, for example, recalls Clytaemnestra in the *Agamemnon:*

Soon the heart's blood of all I love on earth
Will sprinkle him, and he will wipe it off
As if 'twere only rain.

The murder-scene is Sophoclean:

LUCREZIA. They are about it now.
BEATRICE. Nay, it is done.
LUCREZIA. I have not heard him groan.
BEATRICE. He will not groan.

So is the last scene, with its stress on gentleness, 'fear and pain being subdued' (it is worth comparing with the end of *Samson*). 'Give yourself no unnecessary pain,' she says to the Cardinal: then, to her mother:

Mother, tie
My girdle for me, and bind up my hair
In any simple knot — And yours, I see,
Is coming down. . .

Shelley remembered Euripides' Polyxena, 'very careful of her modesty,' as she fell. He also thinks of Electra's sudden sense of shame at her disorder, when she bade her sister 'Cut a tress of your hair — and this of mine — alas! it is unkempt. . .' But in the *Cenci* the effect depends partly on an earlier scene (Act IV, Scene 1), recalled exactly in the manner of Sophocles. When Beatrice appeared, half-dazed, in her first agony of shame, she said:

How comes this hair undone?
Its wandering strings must be what blind me so,
And yet I tied it fast — O horrible!

X. THE NINETEENTH CENTURY AND AFTER

SINCE the dawn of the nineteenth century Greek Tragedy has been part of the common literary stock, and its influence, though all-pervasive, becomes more and more difficult to analyze. The romantic movement led back both to the Elizabethans and to Greece, away from Latin, not away from the Classics. Wordsworth read Plato.[109] Thanks to Francklin and Potter, Keats knew enough of the *Prometheus* and the *Oedipus at Colonus* to draw inspiration for *Hyperion* from both. Coleridge lectured on Greek Tragedy. Hazlitt, criticizing the contemporary theatre, constantly referred to the Greeks. Beddoes confessed, when he took his degree at Oxford: 'Oxford is the most indolent place on earth. I have done fairly nothing,' but admitted he had read 'a few plays of Schiller, Aeschylus, Euripides.' Incidentally he had been writing the *Bride's Tragedy*. Later on we find Fitzgerald making his English adaptations of the *Oresteia* and the *Oedipus* — ' not meat for scholars, mainly for Mrs. Kemble ' — and stirring up Robert Browning to make a version of the *Agamemnon.* When he saw it he was sorry. Elizabeth Browning's *Prometheus* may not be inspired: anyhow, it is readable: her husband's *Agamemnon* is a fantastic travesty, due in part to the still prevalent misconception of the Titan's uncouth and undisciplined genius. ' Oh, our Aeschylus, the thunderous! How he drove the bolted breath. . .', as Mrs. Browning exclaims in the touching verses which describe her reading of Greek Tragedy with the blind scholar Boyd in Switzerland. Carlyle, of course, imagined and applauded Aeschylus as a vast, hairy giant. Matthew Arnold understood Greek Tragedy far better than any of these. Tennyson — though his ' refreshing of the mind ' [110] with Aeschylus and Sophocles did not make *Harold* into a good play — has some charming echoes: Arthur in *Guinevere,* imagining himself lonely in the hall, like Menelaus dreaming of Helen in the *Agamemnon;* and, in the *Dream of Fair Women,* the vision of Helen, ' stiller than chiselled marble,' with Iphigeneia, in the trancèd, silent wood; and the King, in

The Passing of Arthur, 'looking wistfully, as in a picture,' when he rises to go down to the boat, and Sir Bedivere at the end, looking after him, in silence, revolving memories, like Theseus in the *Oedipus at Colonus.* Stevenson too felt the influence of Sophocles. 'I, the Bohnist, the un-Grecian,' he writes, 'was the means of converting J. A. Symonds in the matter of the *Ajax'*—that is, about the vexed question of the final scenes. 'The resource displayed in the *Oedipus Rex,'* he wrote to Lewis Campbell, 'is a miracle. Voltaire's . . criticisms, which had been fatal to a narrative, do not amount amongst them to exhibit one flaw in this masterpiece of drama. . . For the drama it is perfect.' [111]

Scholars, like Porson and Blomfield, Hermann and K. O. Müller, with their 'various readings, verbal criticisms, etc.,' had done much to clear the text of errors and to make intelligent appreciation possible. At the Universities, whatever their faults may have been, Greek poetry was once more read as poetry. In 1842 a Mr. J. F. Boyes, a Fellow of St. John's College, Oxford, published a collection of modern illustrations to Aeschylus, followed some years later by a less successful collection for Sophocles and Euripides. He records the fact that of late years 'the quickened study of Greek drama' had been accompanied by 'a decided revival of the study of our own old dramatic literature.' He notes the wide influence of the *Prometheus,* and he sees — which was very rare, even among scholars, at that time — that Aeschylus was a master of construction. 'Shelley's abandonment in inspiration is often that of a Pythoness, but even in his obscurity there is something of divine: this is the first impression of Aeschylus. A narrower observation leads me to think that, sublime as was the inspiration, . . he had a self-control, which appears in his choral odes: poetic rage was in reality the effect of the most deliberate study and design.' What Boyes suspected, Weil and Wilamowitz, and, above all, Walter Headlam, have since proved. The proof was made easier by the development of modern music-drama.

The Chorus had been the chief stumbling-block. Fitzgerald made good work of the dialogue, where he divined that Marlowe was the ideal model for translators. The Chorus he could not 'think so fine as people talk of. . . I have always said the Chorus in general was little else than a sort of interact music, of nonsense verse, like an Italian libretto.' For the *Oedipus* he took the desperate measure of printing 'old Potter's versions,' bidding Mrs. Kemble get a hint from them of what the ode was about, and then 'imagine some grand piece of music — say a Prelude of Bach.' That was at any rate an advance on the suggestion of 'nonsense-verses.' But Fitzgerald still thinks of Aeschylus as 'the old Titan . . a rugged mountain, lashed by seas and riven by thunderbolts . . a Gothic cathedral.'[112]

This same uneasiness about the Chorus is reflected in the accounts we have of the *Antigone*, as performed with Mendelssohn's incidental music first in Berlin, then in London, Edinburgh and Dublin. Miss Helen Faucit, who won all hearts as the heroine, records her delight in the work, and her sense that the Irish seemed better qualified to appreciate Greek Tragedy than either the English or the Scots. De Quincey saw her in Edinburgh, and fell in love with her, 'Holy heathen, daughter of God before God was known, flower from Paradise after Paradise was closed'! As for the Chorus, with its 'synagogical chanting,' really, it would not do. 'Think of these worthy men in their white and sky-blue liveries, kept standing the whole evening — no seats allowed, no dancing, no tobacco: nothing to console them but Antigone's beauty: and all this in our climate' (Edinburgh, Dec. 30, 1845).[113]

Meanwhile Wagner was learning how to link the forms of music in a new and fruitful union with dramatic words and action; and his work was directly inspired by Aeschylus. At school, he says, he had paid only just as much attention to his Classics as was absolutely necessary 'to enable me to get a grasp.' 'Greek particularly attracted me . . the grammar seemed merely a tiresome obstacle. . .' As a youth, he had slept when Uncle Adolph read his German version of the *Oedipus* aloud. The wise old man did not rebuke him. His first operas were in the old grand style in which music and drama are not organically one. But in 1847, at the age of thirty-four, 'I was impelled,' he says, 'by my spiritual needs to turn my attention once more to that all-important source of culture' (Greek dramatic poetry). 'For the first time I now mastered Aeschylus with real feeling and understanding. . . Nothing could equal the sublime emotion with which the Trilogy inspired me, and to the last words of the *Eumen-*

ides I lived in an atmosphere so far removed from the present day that I have never since been really able to reconcile myself with modern literature. My ideas about the whole significance of the drama and of the theatre were, without a doubt, moulded by these impressions.' He worked at *Lohengrin* in the morning and read Greek plays in the afternoon in his shrubbery.[114]

The result was opera of a new kind, in which the drama never ceased to be musical, the music to be dramatic. The old opera as a rule (there are qualifications to be made, of course: Glück, for instance, set a good example) had consisted either of musical numbers interrupting a play, or of musical oases linked by dreary recitative. In Greek drama, which arose from choral lyric, the spoken word, as we have seen, never quite lost its musical relation to the rest of the performance. Wagner went back to the Greek tradition not only by insisting that the composer ought strictly to be the author of the words, the dictator of the gestures and the designer even of the stage-setting, but also in his conception of the whole performance as one musical-dramatic composition, and in his rediscovery of the dramatic *Leit-Motif*. Only, of course, he had the vastly greater resources of the modern orchestra for his musical effects, and the relation between his comparatively childish verbal technique and his elaborately orchestrated music reverses the Greek order of importance. In Aeschylus the instrumental music and the singing must have been comparatively simple: the verbal element was the more complex and the more elaborate in structure.

In these matters, since the middle of last century, scholars, poets and musicians have travelled hand in hand. Just as Wagner's treatment of opera made it easier for Headlam to discover and expound the main principles on which the Aeschylean trilogy is built, so Swinburne's metrical experiments, consciously inspired by the Greek odes, though based on no very accurate knowledge of their systems, have made the Aeschylean and Sophoclean metres far more intelligible to English ears.[115] A sure instinct led Professor Murray to adopt Swinburnian metres for his versions of the lyrics in Euripides. There is indeed a certain pleasing irony in his success. Swinburne himself indignantly repelled suggestions that he was indebted to the 'scenic sophist.' 'As far as *Erechtheus* can be said to be formed after anybody, it is modelled throughout on the earlier style of Aeschylus . . the style most radically contrary to the droppings, grrh! the droppings (as our divine and dearest Mrs. Browning so aptly rather than delicately puts it) of the scenic sophist that can be conceived.' Mr. Drinkwater misses in Swinburne rhythmical, as distinct from metrical subtlety. That is not, perhaps, surprising. It does not follow that 'the introduction of classical metres into English poetry is a lost cause.' After all, in experimental work it is natural that the metrical beat should predominate: the subtler rhythmical harmonies may come later. Mr. Trevelyan's scholarly work, for instance, is at present only half successful, precisely because he is so bent on reproducing faithfully the metrical schemes of the original that he does less than justice to the rhythmical values, the phrasing, which contrast with the metrical analysis. Though it would be absurd to compare Swinburne to Sackville or Mr. Trevelyan to Norton, it is not quite irrelevant to say that *Gorboduc's* jog-trot iambics were harbingers of Marlowe's thunderous blank verse.

Swinburne links modern lovers of Aeschylus and Sophocles with Milton, Landor and Shelley. He loved Landor, as he loved Aeschylus, for 'his passionate compassion, his bitter and burning pity for all wrongs endured in the world.' And he joins the memory of Milton and Shelley with an echo from Aeschylus in his *Litany of Nations:*

> By *the star that Milton's soul for Shelley lighted,*
> W*hose rays ensphere us;*
> By *the beacon-light, repeated, far-off sighted,*
> O *Mother, hear us!*

Like Shelley, Swinburne could not conceive for Zeus 'any future recovery or vindication.' His conception of the gods, free as it was from weakness, lacked the religious profundity of Aeschylus, and the objectiveness of Sophocles. A blind fate triumphs in *Atalanta,* and a cruel set of gods create the conditions in which heroism triumphs, through tragedy, in *Erechtheus.* This is Sophoclean —

> A*t least we witness of thee, ere we die,*
> T*hat these things are not otherwise, but thus* —

But it is more rebellious than Sophocles.

Of the many makers of plays and music who

are still working, this is not the place to speak. One great living writer must be mentioned, whose work has been mainly in prose, but whose imagination is akin to that of Aeschylus, though his vision of life is more like that of Sophocles. Hardy's *Dynasts* would have gained by concentration for the stage. But, as it stands, it is great drama. It is Aeschylean in the wide sweep of its imagination, and the author thought of Aeschylus at the end. After the questioning of the Years and the mocking of the Ironic Spirits, Earth asks, 'What of the Immanent Will?', and the Years reply, 'It works unconsciously as heretofore, Eternal artistries. . .' Then, after the aerial music, and the yearning of the Pities, a stirring fills the air like a sound of joyance 'that the rages of the ages shall be cancelled, and deliverance offered. . . Consciousness the Will informing till it fashion all things fair.' So Prometheus heard the thrilling of the air when the Nymphs came, like a Chorus of Pities, to comfort him. So the *Oresteia* began with the Watchman's prayer for deliverance, and ended with the cancelling of the old rage. Even the phrase 'fashion all things fair' is an echo of the tragic, impossible hope of Clytaemnestra at the end of the *Aga-*

memnon. The conception of the Will, working unconsciously, but in the end, perhaps, attaining consciousness, is a modern echo of the Aeschylean notion that Zeus, who was once young and tyrannical, has been brought by experience to moderation.

Hardy's hope is of the distant future. When he expressed it again in prose, some critics hinted that the master was growing old. So, we are told, the children of Sophocles alleged that in old age he had forgotten how to manage his affairs. He answered by reciting from the *Oedipus at Colonus.* The historians tell us it is not a true story. But poetry is more philosophical than history.

NOTES AND BIBLIOGRAPHY

NOTES

1. *Iliad*, xviii. 590 ff.; *Odyssey*, viii. 260 ff.

2. Cf. J. B. Bury, in *Cambridge Ancient History*, vol. II, Chapter xviii, Cambridge, England, 1924; J. A. Scott, *The Unity of Homer*, Berkeley, California, 1921; J. T. Sheppard, *The Pattern of the Iliad*, London, 1922; cf. "Traces of the Rhapsode," in *The Journal of Hellenic Studies*, xlii. 220–237 (1922).

3. *Poetics*, 1449 a 15–21. Aristophanes, *Frogs*, 1004–5.

4. Aeschylus, *Suppliants*, 98 ff. (a fine verse translation by W. G. Headlam, *Book of Greek Verse*, Cambridge, England, 1907, pp. 73 ff.).

5. Aeschylus, *Fr*. 44, Nauck. Cf. Euripides, *Fr*. 839 and 898; Lucretius, II. 990 ff.; Marcus Aurelius, X. 21. *This, and subsequent translations, if not otherwise described, are by the author.*

6. *Persae*, 293 ff.

7. *Iliad*, xxiv. 527 ff.; *Odyssey*, i. 32 ff.

8. *Agamemnon*, 170 ff.

9. *Prometheus Vinctus*, 88 ff.

10. In accepting the dedication of W. G. Headlam's *Agamemnon*.

11. *Agamemnon*, 1–21 (in full).

12. *Agamemnon*, 22–33 (summary).

13. *Agamemnon*, 34–39.

14. *Agamemnon*, 40–103.

15. *Agamemnon*, 104–269 (249–260 in full).

16. *Agamemnon*, 276–9 and 291.

17. *Agamemnon*, 413–463.

18. *Agamemnon*, 1053 and 1326–9.

19. *Agamemnon*, 1371 ff. For 'I will not blush,' cf. her earlier speech, 846 ff., and Sophocles, *Electra*, 254.

20. *Agamemnon,* 1550–8. Cf. Euripides, *Iphigeneia at Aulis,* 631 ff.

21. *Eumenides,* 341 ff., trs., A. W. Verrall.

22. *Eumenides,* 1029 and 1045–9.

23. Thucydides, II. 35–46.

24. Phrynichus, *The Muses,* Fr. 31 (K. T. Kock, *Comicorum Atticorum Fragmenta,* vol. I. p. 379).

25. *Antigone,* 332 ff.

26. *Antigone,* 450–5. For the legal question, cf. A. C. Pearson, in *Classical Quarterly,* xvi. 130–2 (1922).

27. *Antigone,* 512–523.

28. Aeschylus, *Agamemnon,* 916. The best account of these ideas, and their application in Tragedy is given by W. Headlam, in *Cambridge Praelections,* Cambridge, England, 1906, pp. 99 ff. See also Gilbert Murray, *The Rise of the Greek Epic,* Oxford, 1924, pp. 83–7, and the Introduction to my edition of the *Oedipus Tyrannus,* Cambridge, England, 1920 (Chapter 4).

29. *Ajax,* 133.

30. *Ajax,* 271 ff.

31. *Ajax,* 412–428.

32. *Ajax,* 550 ff.

33. *Ajax,* 646–692. Since this paragraph was written, Dr. G. A. Auden has suggested to me that, in cases of delusional insanity, such a change of purpose as is implied if we interpret this speech as simply true, is not uncommon. The patient is profoundly depressed after recovery, but there may come a moment of complete sanity, followed often by a relapse.

34. Aeschylus, *Libation-Bearers,* 121–2 and 140–5.

35. Sophocles, *Electra,* 239–250.

36. *Electra,* 307.

37. *Electra,* 449 ff. Dr. Pearson, however, thinks that the touch about her hair being 'unkempt' is due to a false reading.

38. *Electra,* 580–3.

39. *Electra,* 616 ff.

40. *Electra,* 770–1.

41. *Electra,* 1398 ff.

42. *Oedipus Tyrannus,* 1512 ff. I have discussed the interpretation of these lines more fully in my edition.

43. *Oedipus Tyrannus,* 1170 ff.; contrast this with Jocasta's story, 717 ff.

44. *Trachiniae,* 21–3, 35, 61–6.

45. *Trachiniae,* 1264 ff.

46. Herodotus, I. 30–32.

47. Cf. F. M. Cornford, *Thucydides Mythistoricus,* London, Edward Arnold, 1907 (with the criticism of J. B. Bury, *The Ancient Greek Historians,* London, 1909).

48. Dio Chrysostom, *Or.* XII, vol. I. p. 220, Dindorf. Cf. Cicero, *Orator,* II. 8; Quintilian, XII. 10. 9.

49. Pausanias, V. 11.

50. *Oedipus Tyrannus,* 863 ff.

51. Plato, *Apology,* 41 C.

52. Plato, *Republic,* III. 401 B. C.

53. *Apology,* 37 E.

54. *Republic,* II. 380 A, 383 B.

55. *Republic,* I. 329 B. C.

56. R. D. Archer Hind, *Plato's Timaeus,* Cambridge, England, 1888, pp. 17–18.

57. Aristophanes, *Clouds,* 1367; Quintilian, X. 66.

58. These, and other anecdotes of this kind will be found in Patin's *Études sur les Tragiques Grecs,* Paris, 1884.

59. Accius, *Agamemnonidae, Fr.* i, Ribbeck, p. 141.

60. Accius, *Philocteta, Fr.* xi, Ribbeck, p. 207.

61. *Fr. Inc.,* lxxii, Ribbeck, p. 254. Cf. Aeschylus, *Eumenides,* 903 ff.

62. Cicero, *Tusculans,* II. 10. 23; *ad Quintum Fratrem,* III. 6 (read 'quereris'); Plutarch, *Pompey,* 78.

63. Lucretius, I. 84–101. Cf. Euripides, *Hecuba,* 518 ff.

64. Horace, *Odes,* III. 11. 35; I. 7. 27; and III. 3. 1–8.

65. Sophocles, *Ajax,* 550; Accius, *Armorum Judicium, Fr.* x, Ribbeck, p. 156; Virgil, *Aeneid,* XII. 435.

66. Ovid, *Tristia,* V. 4. 12; *Ex Ponto,* III. 1. 54. But Ovid borrows more from Euripides (see Lucas, *Euripides and his Influence,* pp. 69 ff.).

67. Tertullian, *Apology,* 9. 29; *de Spectaculis, passim; Marcion,* 1. 1. Cf. Arnobius, *Adversus Gentes,* IV. 35.

68. *Purgatorio,* XII. 37 (cf. Ovid, *Metamorphoses,* VI. 301–2); *Paradiso,* V. 68.

69. Cf. Sandys' *Harvard Lectures,* p. 179.

70. James Elroy Flecker, *The Grecians,* London, 1910, p. 50.

71. W. H. Woodward, *Vittorino da Feltre,* Cambridge, England, 1912, pp. 50 and 68.

72. Vespasiano da Bisticci, quoted by Sandys, *Harvard Lectures,* p. 55.

73. See R. C. Jebb's *Introduction to the Facsimile of the Laurentian MS.,* London, 1885.

74. Jebb, *Text of Sophocles,* Cambridge, England, 1906, p. xxxii.

75. Paris, 1557.

76. Cf. G. Pettina, *Vicenza* (*Italia Artistica,* I. 17), Bergamo, 1922.

77. Rabelais, II. 8.

78. Montaigne, II. 17.

79. P. de Nolhac, *Ronsard et l'Humanisme,* Paris, 1921.

80. de Nolhac, p. 39, gives a specimen. Mr. Lucas (*Euripides and his Influence,* p. 98) finds in his *Hecuba* 'the promise of the sonorous splendours of the century to follow.'

81. M. de Nolhac thinks (*Ronsard,* p. 44) that the alleged edition of 1548 never existed.

82. Du Bellay, *Défense,* quoted by Egger. Cf. Ronsard's Preface to the *Franciade:* 'Learn Greek and Latin diligently . . compose in your mother-tongue.' Good advice, which not all classical scholars have yet adopted.

83. *Antigone,* 227 ff. But cf. Seneca, *Thyestes,* Act III. 423 ff.; Euripides, *Phoenissae,* 363. See, for the whole paragraph, M. Augé-Chiquet, *J-A de Baif,* Paris, 1909.

84. The text of this most interesting play will be found in Viollet le Duc, *Ancien Théâtre Français,* Paris, 1855, vol. 4.

85. Cf. Sophocles, *Oedipus Tyrannus,* 1237 ff.

86. Roger Ascham, *The Scholemaster,* English Works, Cambridge, England, 1904.

87. *Oedipus Coloneus,* 1129.

88. *Oedipus Tyrannus,* 1111–2 (misapplied).

89. In his insistence on the part played by Latin in Grammar-School education, and by the Greek classics in the creation of the general spirit of the time, Churton Collins did good service. For the weakness of his Greek 'parallels,' cf. Lucas, *Euripides,* pp. 107 ff.

90. Boas, p. 92. Cf. G. C. Moore Smith, *College Plays,* Cambridge, England, 1923.

91. The best statement of the probabilities will be found in H. R. D. Anders, *Shakespeare's Books,* Berlin, 1904.

92. Lucas, *Euripides,* p. 19.

93. Cf. Anders, p. 114.

94. See K. Hartfelder, *Philipp Melanchthon als Praeceptor Germaniae,* Leipzig, 1889, and *Melanchthoniana Paedagogica,* Leipzig, 1892 (pp. 92 ff. for Veit Oertel's address). Cf. Koch, *Melanchthons Schola Privata,* Gotha, 1859.

95. O. Dähnhardt, *Griechische Dramen in Deutschen Bearbeitungen,* Stuttgart, 1896–7.

96. Harington's '*Briefe Apologie*' formed the preface to his version of *Orlando Furioso,* 1591. Cf. Milton, *Paradise Regained,* IV. 249 ff.

97. *Art of Poesie,* ascribed to George Puttenham, London, 1589.

98. *Paradise Lost,* I. 197, 287; II. 635, 1040; IV. 15.

99. *Paradise Regained,* I. 222. Cf. *Eumenides,* 830 ff., 882, 971 and *passim.*

100. *Paradise Regained,* II. 417. Cf. *Oedipus Tyrannus,* 542.

101. Patin, vol. II. p. 159.

102. Duport's book appeared as early as 1660, but was long popular. Johnson's Eton editions of the Tragic poets (beginning in 1706) marked a great advance in school teaching.

103. *Joseph Andrews,* specially II. 11 and III. 1.

104. *Oedipus Tyrannus,* 629.

105. By Dr. Godley, I think.

106. W. B. Drayton Henderson, *Swinburne and Landor,* London, 1918, gives details about the influence of Greek Tragedy on both poets.

107. *Agamemnon,* 755 ff. is the starting-point: the reconciliation of the Furies by Athena is the solution.

108. Sophocles, *Electra,* 307, 451, 445 (cf. Aeschylus, *Agamemnon,* 1388), 616 ff.

109. J. Adam, *The Vitality of Platonism,* Cambridge, England, 1911, seems to me to prove this.

110. Cf. W. P. Mustard, *Classical Echoes in Tennyson,* Columbia Studies in English III, New York, 1904.

111. S. Colvin, *Memories and Notes,* London, 1921, p. 133; Stevenson, *Works,* London, 1912, vol. xxiv. pp. 113–4.

112. Fitzgerald, *Letters,* Aldis Wright, Cambridge, England, 1887, vol. L, pp. 190, 259, 294, 360 (on his *Agamemnon,* 'better a live dog than a dead lion in drama'). In 1880 he dedicated his *Oedipus* to Charles Eliot Norton. He was much interested in the Harvard Greek play. In 1881 he wrote to Norton that 'thirty years ago' he had begged W. H. Thompson to organize a Greek play in the Senate House at Cambridge, 'but our Cambridge is too well-fed and slow to stir.' In 1882 came the Cambridge *Ajax,* but he did not see it. See also *Letters to Fanny Kemble,* London, 1895, p. 208, and *More Letters,* London, 1902, p. 196.

113. de Quincey, *Works,* Masson, Edinburgh, 1890, vol. X. pp. 346 ff. For an amusing comment on the London performance, as well as an account of Classical studies in England at this time, see C. A. Bristed, *Five Years at an English University* [3], London and New York, 1873.

114. Richard Wagner, *Autobiography,* Engl. translation, '*Of My Life,*' London, 1911, vol. I. pp. 15 and 411 ff. Wagner's method also owes something to Grillparzer; but that points back again to Aeschylus. The dramatic romance of the Fleece-motif in the Medea trilogy recalls that of the robe-motif in the *Oresteia.* Maeterlinck in our own time carried on the tradition. The Hofmannstal-Strauss *Electra* has little or no affinity with Classical plays.

115. See the interesting letter from Swinburne in Mr. Cecil Headlam's *Memoir of W. G. Headlam,* London, 1910, pp. 61–2.

BIBLIOGRAPHY

ANDERS, H. R. D., *Shakespeare's Books*. Berlin, 1904.

BOAS, F. S., *University Drama in the Tudor Age*. Oxford, 1914.

CAMPBELL, LEWIS, *Tragic Drama in Aeschylus, Sophocles and Shakespeare*. London, 1904.

COLLINS, J. CHURTON, *Matthew Arnold's Merope and Sophocles' Electra*. Oxford, 1906.

——, *Studies in Shakespeare*. New York, 1904.

CREIZENACH, WILHELM M. A., *Geschichte des neueren Dramas*. 5 vols. Halle a S., 1893–1916. (Translation, by C. Hugon, *The English Drama in the Age of Shakespeare*, London and Philadelphia, 1916.)

CUNLIFFE, J. W., *Early English Classical Tragedies*. Oxford, 1912.

EGGER, A. E., *L'hellénisme en France*. Paris, 1869.

FLICKINGER, R. C., *The Greek Theater and Its Drama* [2]. Chicago, 1922.

GOODELL, T. D., *Athenian Tragedy*. New Haven, 1920.

HAIGH, A. E., *The Attic Theatre* [3] (revised by A. W. Pickard-Cambridge). Oxford, 1907.

——, *The Tragic Drama of the Greeks*. Oxford, 1896.

HEINEMANN, KARL, *Die Tragischen Gestalten der Griechen in der Weltliteratur*, in the Series: *Das Erbe der Alten*. 2 vols. Leipzig, 1920.

LENTILHAC, E., *de J. C. Scaligeri Poetice*. Paris, 1887.

LUCAS, F. L., *Seneca and Elizabethan Tragedy*. Cambridge, England, 1922.

——, *Euripides and His Influence*, in the Series: *Our Debt to Greece and Rome*. Boston, 1923.

MACKAIL, J. W., Essay on 'Sophocles,' in *Lectures on Greek Poetry*. London and New York, 1911.

MUELLER, A., *Das Griechische Drama u. Seine Wirkung bis zur Gegenwart*. Kempfen u. Munich, n.d.

MUELLER, H. F., *Beiträge zum Verständniss der Tragischen Kunst*. Wolfenbüttel, 1909.

MURRAY, GILBERT, 'Greek and English Tragedy,' in G. S. Gordon (editor), *English Literature and the Classics*. Oxford, 1912.

PATIN, H. J. G., *Études sur les Tragiques Grecs, Eschyle* [7]. Paris, 1890.

——, *Études sur les Tragiques Grecs, Sophocle* [12]. Paris, 1896.

RIBBECK, OTTO, *Scaenicae Romanorum Poesis Fragmenta*. 2 vols. Vol. I. *Tragicorum Romanorum Fragmenta* [2]. Lipsiae, 1871.

SANDYS, J. E., *Harvard Lectures on the Revival of Learning*. Cambridge, England, 1905.

SHEPPARD, J. T., *Greek Tragedy* (Cambridge Manuals). Cambridge, England, 1911.

SMYTH, H. WEIR, *Aeschylean Tragedy*. Berkeley, California, and Cambridge, England, 1924.

SYMONDS, J. A., Essay on 'Aeschylus,' in *Studies of the Greek Poets*. London, 1902.

VERRALL, A. W., *Lectures on Dryden*. Cambridge, England, 1914.

AESCHYLUS

Greek Text:

SIDGWICK, A., *Aeschyli Tragoediae*. 2 vols. Oxonii, 1899.

WEIL, H., *Aeschyli Tragoediae*. Lipsiae, 1907.

WILAMOWITZ-MOELLENDORFF, U. VON, *Aeschyli Tragoediae*. Berlin, 1914.

Greek and English:

SMYTH, H. WEIR, *Aeschylus, with an English Translation*, in *The Loeb Classical Library*. 2 vols. New York and London, Vol. I. 1922; Vol. II. 1926. (Full bibliography of editions and translations.)

Greek and French:

MAZON, PAUL, *Eschyle*, in the *Collection . . . de l'Association G. Budé*. 2 vols. Paris, 1920–1925.

BIBLIOGRAPHY

English translations:

HEADLAM, WALTER G., and C. E. S., *The Plays of Aeschylus* (prose version). London, 1909.

WAY, A. S., *Aeschylus,* in English Verse. 3 vols. London and New York, 1906–1908.

Separate plays (in verse translation):

BEVAN, E. R., *The Prometheus.* London, 1902.

HEADLAM, W. G., *The Agamemnon.* Cambridge, England, 1910. (Edited by A. C. Pearson.)

COOKSON, G. M., *Four Plays.* Oxford, 1922.

COOKSON, G. M., *The Oresteia.* Oxford, 1924.

TREVELYAN, R. C., *The Oresteia.* Liverpool, 1922. (Acting edition, with Greek text, Cambridge, England, 1920.)

MURRAY, GILBERT, *The Agamemnon.* London, n.d.

——, *The Choëphoroe.* Oxford, 1923.

——, *The Eumenides.* Oxford, 1926.

(R. Browning, *The Agamemnon,* Mrs. Browning, *The Prometheus.*)

SOPHOCLES

Greek Text:

JEBB, R. C., *Text of Sophocles.* Cambridge, England, 1906.

PEARSON, A. C., *Sophoclis Fabulae.* Oxonii, 1924.

Greek and English:

JEBB, R. C., *Sophocles, The Plays and Fragments* (with critical notes, commentary, and translation into English prose). 7 vols. Cambridge, England, 1885–1896.

STORR, F., *Sophocles, with an English Translation,* in *The Loeb Classical Library.* 2 vols. New York and London, 1919. (Full bibliography of editions and translations.)

Greek and French:

MASQUERAY, PAUL, *Sophocle,* in the *Collection . . de l'Association G. Budé.* 2 vols. Paris, 1922–1924.

English translations:

JEBB, R. C., *The Tragedies of Sophocles* (prose version). Cambridge, England, 1905. (Reprinted in one volume from the large edition.)

WAY, A. S., *Sophocles,* in English Verse. 2 vols. London, 1909–1914.

BIBLIOGRAPHY

Separate plays (in verse translation):

WHITELAW, R., *Sophocles,* in English Verse. London, 1904.

MURRAY, GILBERT, *Oedipus, King of Thebes.* Oxford, 1911.

TREVELYAN, R. C., *The Ajax.* London, 1919.

——, *The Antigone.* London, 1925.

SHEPPARD, J. T., *The Oedipus Tyrannus of Sophocles* (translated and explained). Cambridge, England, 1920.

[The editors have taken the liberty of adding reference to: Moody, Wm. Vaughn, *The Fire-Bringer.* Boston, 1904; Spitteler, Karl, *Prometheus der Dulder.* Jena, 1924; Wilson, Pearl Cleveland, *Wagner's Dramas and Greek Tragedy.* New York, 1919.]

Our Debt to Greece and Rome

AUTHORS AND TITLES

AUTHORS AND TITLES

HOMER. *John A. Scott.*

SAPPHO. *David M. Robinson.*

EURIPIDES. *F. L. Lucas.*

ARISTOPHANES. *Louis E. Lord.*

DEMOSTHENES. *Charles D. Adams.*

THE POETICS OF ARISTOTLE. *Lane Cooper.*

GREEK RHETORIC AND LITERARY CRITICISM. *W. Rhys Roberts.*

LUCIAN. *Francis G. Allinson.*

CICERO AND HIS INFLUENCE. *John C. Rolfe.*

CATULLUS. *Karl P. Harrington.*

LUCRETIUS AND HIS INFLUENCE. *George Depue Hadzsits.*

OVID. *Edward Kennard Rand.*

HORACE. *Grant Showerman.*

VIRGIL. *John William Mackail.*

SENECA THE PHILOSOPHER. *Richard Mott Gummere.*

APULEIUS. *Elizabeth Hazelton Haight.*

MARTIAL. *Paul Nixon.*

PLATONISM. *Alfred Edward Taylor.*

ARISTOTELIANISM. *John L. Stocks.*

STOICISM. *Robert Mark Wenley.*

LANGUAGE AND PHILOLOGY. *Roland G. Kent.*

AUTHORS AND TITLES

AESCHYLUS AND SOPHOCLES. *J. T. Sheppard.*

GREEK RELIGION. *Walter Woodburn Hyde.*

SURVIVALS OF ROMAN RELIGION. *Gordon J. Laing.*

MYTHOLOGY. *Jane Ellen Harrison.*

ANCIENT BELIEFS IN THE IMMORTALITY OF THE SOUL. *Clifford H. Moore.*

STAGE ANTIQUITIES. *James Turney Allen.*

PLAUTUS AND TERENCE. *Gilbert Norwood.*

ROMAN POLITICS. *Frank Frost Abbott.*

PSYCHOLOGY, ANCIENT AND MODERN. *G. S. Brett.*

ANCIENT AND MODERN ROME. *Rodolfo Lanciani.*

WARFARE BY LAND AND SEA. *Eugene S. McCartney.*

THE GREEK FATHERS. *James Marshall Campbell.*

GREEK BIOLOGY AND MEDICINE. *Henry Osborn Taylor.*

MATHEMATICS. *David Eugene Smith.*

LOVE OF NATURE AMONG THE GREEKS AND ROMANS. *H. R. Fairclough.*

ANCIENT WRITING AND ITS INFLUENCE. *B. L. Ullman.*

GREEK ART. *Arthur Fairbanks.*

ARCHITECTURE. *Alfred M. Brooks.*

ENGINEERING. *Alexander P. Gest.*

MODERN TRAITS IN OLD GREEK LIFE. *Charles Burton Gulick.*

ROMAN PRIVATE LIFE. *Walton Brooks McDaniel.*

GREEK AND ROMAN FOLKLORE. *William Reginald Halliday.*

ANCIENT EDUCATION. *J. F. Dobson.*